Hunting Together

Through Motivation-Based Training

Predation Substitute Training – Volume 1

Second Edition

Simone Mueller

Foreword by Claire Staines
Contributions by Lhanna Dickson and
Charlotte Garner
Illustrations by Päivi Kokko

Hunting Together! Harnessing Predatory Chasing in Family Dogs through Motivation-Based Training has provided the most accurate information possible. The techniques and training protocols used in this manual are state-of-the-art among science-based, force-free dog trainers and behaviourists who specialize in force-free anti-predation Training. The author shall not be held liable for any damages resulting from use of this book.

Impressum:
Simone Mueller
Pattbergstrasse 15
74867 Neunkirchen
Germany

Table of Contents

Foreword

As a "reward-based trainer" who seeks to use functional rewards for a plethora of behaviours, I have always found dogs with a huge chase drive a struggle. Then I came across my now dear friend and esteemed colleague Simone Mueller.

Simone introduced me to "Predation Substitute Training". Not a new concept, as Gundog trainers across the globe are able to harness their dog's desire to hunt and use it to their advantage. Not one single Gundog trainer I know wishes to dilute their dog's hunt instinct, they nurture and grow it like a fabulous garden, yet they have complete control of when to turn it on and off. How can we get a pet dog owner to this level?

We must admit that dogs worrying wildlife and livestock is an issue. Every owner fears that their dog can potentially harm another animal and have their dog lose their life in the process.

The protocols, games and concepts that Simone uses do just that! Instead of being the killjoy that says, "you can't be doing that, Fido", preventing their dog from doing the thing they were engineered for. Instead, this allows you, the dog's caregiver, to step into that box with your dog and be the person that says, "Let's do it together, Fido". How cool is that!?

There are lots of ideas from dogs who love scenting, dogs who love ripping, dogs who love chasing and dogs who love stalking! A guide into "which category is your dog in" this can be due to genetics, past experiences and just what floats your dog's boat.

I have since switched to this concept with my own Rhodesian Ridgebacks; in the past, I spent so much time teaching, building and rehearsing a stellar recall, which I have to admit worked; however, I wasn't fooling myself that being called away from a squirrel was more than a little disappointing for the Lion Hounds and took an epic amount of effort to teach and maintain. Learning to turn that on its head and teaching my dogs to slow down that natural Salsa dance that is predation, watching my dogs savour every second of the sight and scent of the forest, watching them slowly stalk and sometimes point the wildlife out to me, to then standing still with every muscle poised ready to unleash their inner ancestry has been a deal breaker for us! I have no doubt in my mind that my dogs love being in that moment, and I get to share it with them.

Simone's insight into a dog's mind is breathtaking. Our many chats on this topic have gone down well with a Gin or two.

I will never forget the moment when working with Simone and my Ridgeback, Tiger, when Tiger was quietly watching a deer, the deer watching her, these two species drinking one another in, and then after what felt like a lifetime, the deer slowly approached us, Tiger didn't move and the two, dog and deer, ended off nose to nose in a moment's pause. Separated only by a mesh gate, neither seemed threatened by the other, casually checking one another out. When the deer turned and trotted off Tiger turned to Simone and me as if to say, "did you see that!?" it was only then Simone, and I dared to breathe!

I hope that you enjoy this book and get as much out of it as I have.

Claire Staines
PCT–A
VSPDT

Tiger

Introduction

Living With A Dog That Loves To Hunt

Does this situation sound all too familiar?

Your dog is sniffing the ground and does not respond to any of your desperate attempts to call them back. Suddenly, they stop. They have spotted a rabbit across the field. Off they go on a wild chase! You're left standing in the middle of the field, shouting and whistling in vain. In your chest, you feel a persistent fear that they'll end up darting across a busy road, or cross paths with an angry farmer or trigger-happy hunter.

Finally, after what feels like an eternity, your dog comes back with a huge canine smile across their face. Their eyes are gleaming with joy, and their whole body communicates excitement, trying to convey to you that this little unplanned jaunt WAS AMAZING! You, on the other hand, are just glad they have returned without a scratch.

In 2002, during the time I spent with my then-first dog Malinka, this scenario - the dashing, the worrying, the frustration and the relief after the reunion - was all too familiar to me.

Malinka was a gorgeous black mixed breed dog – half Australian Shepherd and a dash of various other breeds to keep things interesting. I quickly noticed that she was passionate about chasing wildlife into the woods on our walks. Whether or not there was actual wildlife on her radar or just a suspect sniff or twig snap, she was always poised to race to find the culprit. She seemed to live for the hunt, forever hopeful that a chase was on the horizon.

In most conventional training protocols, the human (i.e. me) ends up as the annoying factor that ruins the fun. These methods generally work by interrupting and stopping the dog's predatory behaviour, often by using a form of punishment. These punishments can include using a shock collar, a spray bottle, or even just recalling them and putting on a leash. All of these things end your dog's fun – they're not welcome, and your dog will quickly resent them – and you. That's because every one of these punishment-based methods works against the nature of our dogs and what they really want: to go for a hunt!

In my case with Malinka, I realised pretty quickly that harsh punishment was not something that I wanted to use with her. In order to give her an outlet for all her predatory energy, I started to play games with her that would mimic the predatory behaviour that she loved to perform. Over the years, I modified some of the games, learned new ones from like-minded trainers, and eventually evolved them into tools for clients' dogs that showed the same hunting enthusiasm my Malinka did. That effort spurred me to create this book, in order to share these effective games-as-training techniques with you.

My training methods are easy to implement into your everyday life, making them an efficient way to bring your dog's chasing behaviours "to heel." I'm confident that they will give your dog, as they did for Malinka and my clients' dogs, a safe outlet for predatory energy without the chasing, dashing, and worrying. The guidance in this book is free from coercion and punishment, and instead uses fun games that correct unwanted behaviours while actually improving your relationship with your dog.

Playing Predation Substitute Games stopped Malinka from running off and searching for wildlife to chase. She focused on me during our walks, always eagerly waiting for me to call her to play her beloved Predation Substitute Games. However, one persistent problem remained. Try as I might, she was never able to resist a good chase when opportunity knocked in the shape of a deer, rabbit or cat. For Malinka and me, our breakthrough moment would take years to manifest, and it was only through learning and using Predation Substitute Training that I was finally able to curb the behaviour.

What Is Predation Substitute Training?

The term "Predation Substitute Training" (PST) has a double meaning. It implies that, through playing Predation Substitute Games with your dog, you'll be able to redirect predatory urges into a harmless owner-centric game, ensuring that predatory energy is released in a safe and controlled way.

The real game-changer, however, is in the deeper meaning of the term. Predation Substitute Training equips you with Predation Substitute Tools. Instead of interrupting your dog's predatory behaviour and ending the fun, you train your dog to perform a safe part of the predatory sequence instead of an unsafe part. E.g., instead of letting them chase, you let them stalk wildlife. This will still let them do what they want to do. In short, hunt!

I have been successfully using this protocol for several years now. Nanook, my 10-year-old Australian Shepherd, used to be a big chaser. Through PST, he has become a passionate visual stalker. Rather than physically taking chase, he's now able to happily sit down and visually follow a running deer in the field while staying by my side.

While it's worked out very well for both my own dogs and my client's dogs, I want to stress something important before we get too deep into practice and theory. Predation Substitute Training is not a quick fix that will stop your dog from chasing. Like most proven dog training techniques, it's hard work and will require a lot of effort to put into your everyday walks to introduce and reinforce concepts. That being said, the positive outcomes that grow from this fair, motivation-centred and need-oriented training are amazing. Once PST has been successfully implemented, your dog will be more controllable in the presence of wildlife. They will be more likely to react to your recall, sharing the joy of performing safe parts of the predatory sequence with you.

Make no mistake about it: predation is pure happiness for our dogs! Imagine using that feeling of pleasure, fulfillment and motivation our dogs find in predation to enforce useful training and deepen your bond with your dog. It's not only possible, but it's also a smart move!

In this training program, you'll find all of the training techniques and tools that you'll need to successfully harness your dog's predatory instincts - all without using intimidation, pain or fear:

- You will understand what predation is and why your dog loves hunting so much.
- You will have Predation Substitute Tools at hand to functionally reinforce your dog in the presence of wildlife. Allowing them to stop and control themselves instead of chasing after game.
- You will be equipped with several need-oriented Predation Substitute Games to create a safe outlet for your dog's predatory energy.

- And you will be provided with a safety net to interrupt unwanted predatory chasing with an emergency cue.

All I ask from you is that you keep an open mind while learning this motivation-centred, science-based approach, and (of course) that you have fun with your dog.

So grab your treat pouch, stuff it with delicious dog treats, and dig out your dog's most exciting toys. It's time to get started!

Why Is Predation Such A Tough Nut To Crack?

First of all, for our dog's ancestors, predation was the only means of survival. Even though our dogs are typically given their bowl of food twice a day, their genes still drive them to hunt for survival. This behaviour is an intrinsic motivator that we have no control over, just like our own needs for water, food, and safety.

This also leads to the second reason why the behaviour is so persistent: predation is genetically anchored: it won't go away. Your dog will not grow out of it when they mature nor can it be fixed by simply spaying or neutering your dog. Genetically-anchored behaviour is super-strong and very hard to interrupt; getting rid of it isn't an option, but guiding it is.

Predation is perfected through learning and experience. Our dogs become more successful at predation through rehearsal. With that in mind, does that mean that they should never have the opportunity to perform predatory behaviour? The answer is both yes and no. Yes, they should be prevented from doing so solo while they're out and about with you, but they should also be allowed to perform safe parts of predation in a controlled, safe environment. All the rigid prevention in the world won't stop your dog from practising predation, anyway: it's such a deeply-rooted behaviour that it can never be "switched off" entirely.

Performing predatory behaviour is an intrinsic need and motivator that our dogs have, regardless of age or breed. Problem-solving, foraging, and hunting-related behaviours are hard-wired to a part of our dog's brain that neuroscientist and psychobiologist Jaak Panksepp called the SEEKING-System. SEEKING is a core emotional system that helps our dogs find resources. The SEEKING-system is also linked to anticipation. When it is activated, our dogs are anticipating something good is about to happen, and they remember how great this makes them feel. In a similar way to humans who enjoy gambling, it's the thrill of the potential win that keeps them coming back for more. This is why the SEEKING-System often takes over our dog's priorities and makes it more challenging for them to think about anything else. If we do not offer our dogs acceptable SEEKING opportunities, they are likely to engage in unwanted behaviours instead.

Some dogs feel this need to hunt stronger than others, and completely suppressing it is like pressing a lid down on a pot of boiling water: it only increases the pressure. These dogs will find an outlet for this pressure, either by going hunting alone or by developing an outlet in other areas, such as chasing bikes, stalking the cat, or destroying the sofa.

This happens because, as an intrinsic motivator, predation feels good! Neurotransmitters, such as dopamine and adrenaline, are released into the dog's body that have the same effect as drugs. The combination of these two neurotransmitters puts our dogs into a euphoric state. To put it bluntly, predation makes our dogs feel high, and it has a similar effect as when humans take drugs.

Even though wolves take up a large number of failed chases, they continue doing this behaviour for these very reasons. Simply ignoring predation, or trying to prevent it completely, will not make it go away!

It's important to remember that the predatory sequence is triggered by visual, auditory and olfactory stimuli in a dog's environment. All our dog's senses are involved in this super intense experience, and this fact can later be used to your advantage.

Why I Choose Not To Use "Aversives"

Is it really possible to harness such strong predation behaviour without the use of aversive techniques - those intended to hurt or scare the dog?

Most dog owners use aversives, such as an e-collar, a spray collar, or discs/rattle bottles, in the best interest of the dog, to protect them from harm. In the end, we all love our dogs and don't want to inflict serious pain or fear on them.

If you use these tools as punishment in your dog's training, Predation Substitute Training can help you to reduce their use and eventually to abandon them altogether. If you use a balanced punishment/praise approach to dog training rather than force-free methods, PST will help you better understand your dog and obtain obedience that your dog gives freely rather than out of fear of reprisal.

Another factor to consider is that when a dog is in full predation mode, there is a neurotransmitter, known as Acetylcholine released, which is responsible for lowering our dog's pain perception. This is why you may see a hunting dog that has been severely wounded by a wild boar or a stag, for example, continuing to hunt even though they have received terrible injuries. Even though these wounds are severe, the dog won't feel the full intensity of the pain whilst they are in full predation mode, and they will simply push through and carry on.

This is why when someone suggests using an e-collar to control your dog's predation because 'the collar only creates a tingle and this isn't painful for your dog,' we now know that this cannot be scientifically possible. In order to be in with a chance of successfully interrupting predatory behaviour when your dog is in full predation mode, there would need to be an extremely high and intense level of pain being inflicted onto them through the e-collar. Even then, because of the euphoric state your dog is in whilst hunting, it's unlikely to stop them completely. This is a damaging cycle to enter because if not done one hundred percent correctly, it will result in you using increasing amounts of force, violence, and pain in an attempt to stop your dog from hunting. This will not only be unsuccessful, but it will also damage the relationship you share with your dog.

Using aversive measures to stop chasing behaviours may be tempting for us, as these tools are easy to use and apparently immediately effective. However, there is a considerable risk that it can all go terribly wrong, as well.

Here are some reasons why I choose not to use aversives in my training:

First of all, your timing needs to be spot on. Are you one hundred percent sure that you captured the moment your dog was looking at the cat in the street, and not the child next to the cat? Your dog will link the pain that he is feeling with the stimulus that he is looking at – that is how dogs learn, through building associations. If the consequences are painful, scary or harmful, learning can occur in a single pairing of a response and a stimulus, a process known as "one-trial learning". Think of it like touching a hot stove for the first time - you won't consciously repeat that mistake, because now you associate the appearance of a flame or red burner with pain. Imagine now that your timing was wrong with that correction for your dog, and they now believe you're punishing them for looking at the child, not the cat. The risk that he will either start to hate children now or become deeply afraid of them is very real.

Second, according to learning theory, the punishment of your dog must be sufficiently hard to endure in order to keep them from ever performing that behaviour again. If you are too hesitant to inflict real fear and real pain on your dog, they will learn to push through the pain or disruption and do it anyway. Once your dog has learned that they can push through the pain, you will find yourself in an infinite spiral of violence against your dog. That's incredibly damaging to both you and your dog.

Third, in classical conditioning, we always condition emotions together with a stimulus and the response. This is the so-called conditioned emotional response (CER). Even if your timing with correction was perfect, your dog might associate the pain, fear and frustration that they experienced when being punished with the stimulus that they saw in that very moment. So instead of chasing the cat they spotted for excitement, their emotions change, and they now experience fear or rage when seeing a cat. They may even try to kill the cat the next time they catch it, because it became the "enemy who shocked them".

Fourth, if you fail to build a clear association between the stimulus and punishment, you run the risk that your dog will never want to work with you again. If you are working your dog in agility, in gun dog trials, or even some simple trick training at home, he may be wary of your intentions in the future. Using pain or fear to get a dog to exhibit a behaviour is counterproductive: the shock tells the dog 'that was wrong' but it doesn't tell the dog what is right, either. By communicating in this way, you are missing out on opportunities to build reinforcement history into that new behaviour, making it enjoyable for the dog to perform. Our dogs do not know about the circumstances that we regard as right or wrong; a behaviour is just a behaviour to them – there is reinforcement that we have built, be it positive or negative, or intrinsic reinforcement. We run the risk of the dog developing anxieties around training, which could lead to sensitisation, psychosomatic stress, and illnesses such as skin conditions, self-damaging behaviour, stomach problems, etc.

It's also worth mentioning that shock collars have been banned in countries such as; Denmark, Norway, Sweden, Austria, Switzerland, Slovenia, Germany, Wales, France, Quebec, and parts of Australia, because they go against animal welfare law. In short, using pain, intimidation and fear in dog training is unethical. Personally, that's not the way I would ever choose to treat my best friend and family member if there are less invasive alternatives.

As dog owners, we need to come up with more creative ideas to harness predation and use them to work together as canine and human, not adversaries.

Take a minute to reflect; what have YOU tried so far to harness your dog's hunting behaviour?

Were these measures effective? Did they influence the relationship with your dog? Even though you are improving and changing your training techniques, weighing past successes and failures will help your first steps of PST proceed more successfully.

New Ways Of Dealing With Predatory Behaviour & How To Use Them

The following process allows you to engage with your dog's predatory behaviour, successfully redirecting it into constructive bonding with you. It uses motivation as a reinforcer and consists of four aspects, each one as important as the next. It's crucial to cover each aspect equally because if you leave out one part, the protocol will not be as effective.

1. **Management and Prevention** – implement general management and training techniques into your daily walks. Your dog will be calmer and more focused on you when out and about. The aim is to teach your dog to stay in contact with you, instead of trying to do everything on their own. This will become second nature and is something that should always be encouraged. While it's unrealistic to have your dog remaining at your side constantly, it's important to encourage them to check in with you regularly. So, they are allowed to go and sniff, which is crucial for their well-being and mental health, but they should check in with you also. This can help reduce their predatory behaviour, because you are closer to them and, therefore, more able to intervene faster. If you can successfully teach your dog how to work with you in areas of low distractions, then it's more likely they will choose to work with you when there are distractions too.

2. **Performing safe parts of the predatory sequence with Predation Substitute Tools** – use these tools in real-life situations whenever you come across wildlife at a distance from which your dog is still in a thinking state. If they are still able to respond to your cues and listen to you, then this is the time to implement predation substitute tools.

3. **Creating an outlet through Predation Substitute Games** – play one or two of these games daily for three to five minutes to meet your dog's innate canine needs.

4. **Creating a safety net by building a super strong "emergency cue" that immediately interrupts unwanted predatory chasing.** – practice the emergency cue at least once a week to be prepared for unexpected encounters with wildlife. This emergency cue can then be used when you encounter something unexpected, or something appears very quickly. An example could be a cat running out from underneath a parked car you are walking past. Or, a squirrel running up a tree very close to you. Basically, when you are in a situation where your dog is no longer able to think clearly, you need to use this emergency cue and create a safe distance between you and the wildlife so your dog can think clearly again.

In another of my books, 'Rocket Recall' we look in depth at how to teach your dog a super strong recall which is used in situations where your dog is off leash, a fair distance away from you and they begin to chase an animal that has suddenly appeared. This special type of recall is designed to get your dog to abort their chasing mission and return back to you. Teaching your dog this can be complex, hence why there is a separate book dedicated to it. So, I will not go into great detail about this here, but you can take a sneak peek into Rocket Recall at the end of this book .

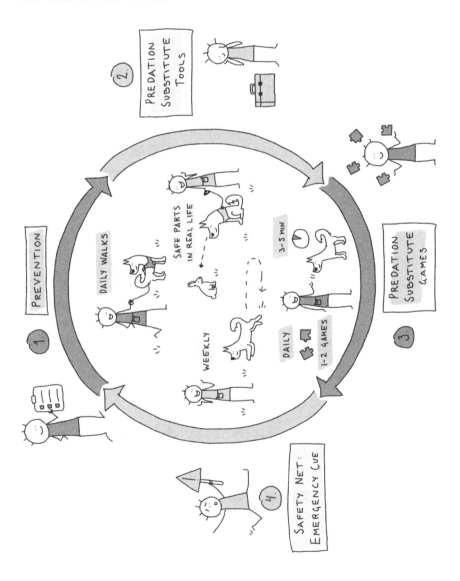

Most conventional training protocols focus merely on the first and the fourth aspects: management and prevention and the interruption of unwanted predatory behaviour. You will need to adopt a more holistic approach for lasting results and real change, rather than simple reactionary behaviour from your dog.

What Are The Perks Of This More Holistic Approach?

First of all, Predation Substitute Training allows you to engage your dog physically and mentally, utilising their daily walks in a way that meets their canine needs. If your dog is allowed to perform safe parts of the predatory sequences regularly, then the desire to hunt solo will be reduced. You will be able to regain control of them in critical situations, such as a deer jumping right onto your path.

As this is a shared activity that is highly rewarding and satisfying for your dog, they also link all the positive feelings with you. Instead of you being the "annoying factor that spoils the fun," you become the "one who enables them to succeed in hunting." This shift in consideration has a marked positive effect on your relationship.

Predation Substitute Training puts the individual parts of the predatory sequence on cue. This gives you diverse, high-quality reward options for your dog that curb wildlife-chasing and improves recalling success.

So What Can PST Look Like In Action?

- Instead of offering a dry biscuit, allow your dog to do what they most like to do at that very moment: let them perform safe parts of predatory behaviour.
- Instead of chasing the rabbit, allow them to stalk the rabbit with their eyes.
- Instead of heading into the woods after a deer, allow them to scent the deer with their nose up.
- Instead of running after the squirrel, let them search for the spot where the squirrel crossed the path and let them show you where it went up the tree.

How To Use This Book

An Important Reminder: the well-being and safety of all animals (wildlife included) takes top priority in this protocol. When dealing with live animals of any size, we have to keep in mind that they all experience emotions, such as panic and fear - even squirrels. They are not objects that we should ever use to train our dogs. As with both dogs and humans, these creatures have a need for safety, and we should respect that at all times!

Who This Book Is Not For

Predation Substitute Training is not designed for use on:

Your Own Pets Or Livestock Who Live At Your Home

Any other domestic pets like cats who live in your home or your own livestock (chickens, sheep, goats etc) that live on your grounds.

PST is unsuitable for these animals because the aim of it isn't to change your dog's perception of the animal they have in front of them. They still view these animals as 'prey', and we do not work against this. And so, we don't want your dog to see your own animals in this way.

However, you can still use the management and prevention techniques, give your dog outlets for their intrinsic predatory needs, teach them solid recall cues, etc., but it's not suitable to use the Predation Substitute Tools in these scenarios.

Animals Who Frequently Visit Your Yard/ Garden

Any wild animals that live in or visit your yard or garden frequently, including squirrels, birds, hedgehogs, etc.

You do not have control over these animals, so management and prevention are a big part of dealing with this effectively.

You could consider fitting window foil to obscure the view of your dog's triggers, so they are not constantly exposed to them. It's also good practice to let your dog out on a leash or go out without the dog and scare away the wildlife before letting your dog outside.

If your dog has the constant anticipation of the chase that waits on the other side of the door, they will never be able to feel calm when they know what may lie ahead of them. The PST protocol is not appropriate for animals in your own yard because:

- The distance between your dog and the wildlife is too small for your dog to remain calm and listen to cues etc.
- Your dog is likely to be showing some level of territorial aggression because the cat/squirrel etc is turning up in their yard over and over again which gets them really wound up and aggravated. Again, this means your dog won't be able to think straight.

- There will be an element of trigger stacking present whereby your dog doesn't have time to calm down and decompress between encountering the wildlife again and again. If your dog is let outside 6 times a day and every time they see wildlife, they will be continually over threshold and even more likely to react negatively towards them.
- The 'Postman Effect', is when a dog barks at the postman (or in this case the animal), and from their viewpoint, they scare the postman (or animal) away. Whereas in reality, the postman is just continuing their deliveries, the bird has flown away or the cat has run off. This success makes the dog feel good and teaches them that it's a good idea to do this again the next time they see this trigger.

This creates an emotional connection for the dog and the postman (or the wildlife); they told them to go away yesterday now here they are again, so the dog gets increasingly annoyed and wound up because they are seemingly ignoring their warnings to leave them alone.

Instead of expecting your dog to be able to keep their cool which is pretty much impossible, throw them a treat party every time the wildlife shows up in the yard.

Never Use PST For Children

It's vital you NEVER use PST for kids. Either your own or children you meet outside regardless of the age of the child. If you are expecting a baby or you already have children at home and your dog wants to chase them, it's important to seek out professional help in this field. Look at www.familypaws.com as a responsible source of information and advice about dogs and children.

Don't Use PST For Other Dogs

For safety's sake, do not allow your dog to stalk other dogs, especially smaller ones! A dog can sometimes get carried away by the emotions and hormones that are released into their body during the predatory sequence. Your dog then might mistake a child or another dog for prey and attempt to grab or even kill it. This phenomenon is called predatory drift, and it can be life-threatening, especially to smaller dogs.

Additionally, another dog may perceive the tense, arrow-shaped body posture of a stalking dog as a threat, and might feel compelled to act aggressively against your dog in defense. If you notice your dog stalking another dog, immediately ask for a check-in from them or recall them as soon as you notice. This helps keep both your pet and others in his environment safe and secure.

PST Shouldn't Be Used To Stop Dogs Chasing Cars

Predation Substitute Training works on the basis that your dog wants to hunt something they perceive as prey. In the case of dogs who want to chase cars, it's unlikely they are chasing them for this reason, it's more likely to be done because they are fearful of the vehicles.

This means that car chasing is actually an example of reactivity, not predation, which is why PST isn't the right method for dealing with this issue.

Most car chasing activity is caused due to the dog feeling startled by a vehicle initially and their fearfulness stems from this encounter. So, if a car suddenly appears, it's likely to trigger the startle response in your dog meaning they want to try and increase the distance between them and the trigger. This is the opposite to predation, which is a distance decreasing activity, where the dog's aim is to get closer to their prey, not further away from it.

So, even though it may look like the dog wants to chase the cars, they are doing this because they want to chase them away through their underlying fearful emotions and not because of predation.

Part 1: Management And Prevention

Management, or the prevention of predatory behaviour, plays an important role in any predation protocol. If you feel that your dog is not trustworthy in certain situations, make sure you do not give them the opportunity to perform unwanted predatory behaviour and put them on a lead.

Equipment

The recommended equipment for this protocol is a three to five-meter leash, attached to a well-fitted harness. A leash that is less than two meters long is not suitable equipment for this need-oriented training, as you'll need to have the ability to provide the distance for later training techniques.

To give your dog more freedom while out and about, a ten-meter long line is a good choice. Never attach a long line to a collar, as the impact of your dog running out the entire length can cause damage or injury to your dog's neck: choose a harness instead.

You also need a market signal or a clicker.

Practical Methods For Management And Prevention

To use management and prevention effectively, your dog needs some basic training. In this part, we often work with treats, for example to teach your dog to regularly orientate to you.

For the work with treats, a marker signal is sometimes used, which corresponds to "clicker training". Since some of the following training sessions assume that you at least know what "clicker training" is, I will devote a short paragraph to it here.

What Is Clicker Training?

Clicker training is a method of telling your dog that they have just performed a desired behaviour by making a sound – in this case a click, but you can also use a word. The sound (word or click) creates a bridge between the behaviour shown and the reward you subsequently give your dog. The sound marks the correct behaviour – not the treat itself, which is given afterwards.

What Are The Advantages Of Clicker Training?

Using a sound to mark correct behaviour has several advantages. A dog has a relatively short period of time in which to associate the reward with their behaviour. If your dog does something right and you reward them with the treat a few seconds later, they may not associate their behaviour with the reward at all – so there is no training effect. In many situations, however, it is not even possible to give the treat immediately when the dog has done something right. For example, your dog may be too far away from you at that moment and has to come to you first to get his treat. Then it is practical if the right moment can first be "marked" by a sound. The dog immediately associates their correct behaviour with the reward through the sound - even if the treat itself comes a little later.

How To Apply Clicker Training?

The most important thing in clicker training is to link the sound with the reward, so that your dog already evaluates the sound as a reward and as something that marks their correct behaviour. Your dog should know: When I hear the click or the marker word, I have done everything right. Therefore, you start clicker training by doing nothing more than making the sound - either a click or you say a certain word - and giving a treat. Important: The sound must ALWAYS be followed by a treat. Even if you clicked by mistake, because your dog cannot recognise your mistake. Once your dog has understood the principle and expects a treat every time you click, you can start to incorporate the click into the training.

A clicker has the advantage that the sound is very precise and your dog can perceive it very well. However, you must always remember to take the clicker with you. Therefore, it makes sense to condition a word instead or in addition. Short, concise words are suitable for this, e.g. "Top" or "Yes".

Since it is not easy for some dogs to take treats outside at all, I dedicate a separate chapter to this problem first. If your dog belongs to the group of dogs that are simply too excited outside to respond to training with treats at all, you will learn how to deal with this here.

In The Mood For Food?

Why Are So Many Dogs Unable To Take Treats Outside?

Many owners become frustrated that their dog is seemingly uninterested in taking treats when they are outside on walks. And some may find this is still the case even when they use the most exciting super treats they can think of! However, something that is often overlooked in these scenarios is the dog's arousal levels. Simply put, the higher the dog's arousal levels are, the less likely they are to show interest in food – no matter how delicious it may be! So, when a dog is in the mood for hunting, their arousal levels are naturally heightened, meaning they simply can't concentrate on food at that moment. However, this can be a problem when it comes to training and responsiveness because a dog that can't find time to eat is unlikely to find time to listen or return to you.

Certain breeds like gundogs and other working breeds are intentionally bred to have higher arousal levels when they're out and about and 'working.' This gives them their keen, alert, focused nature and makes them ideal for the job required of them. So, while this can be helpful when you are asking them to do their intended tasks, it can make it harder for them to concentrate on other things.

Important: The only way to deal with predation in a force-free way and without fear and intimidation is to reduce their arousal to a more manageable level. This

gets the dog's brain into a 'thinking state,' which is crucial for successful learning.

The inability to eat is a closed-circuit problem for dogs. This means they can't eat because their arousal levels are high, and their arousal levels are high because they are stressed because they can't eat. So, it can be impossible to tell what the cause and consequence are in this scenario because one continually leads back to the other and so on. However, it's crucial that you find a way to get your foot into the door of this cycle somehow, to reduce the dog's arousal level and return them to a thinking state where they can eat comfortably.

Although this might sound strange given the situation, you're in; if you can get the dog to eat a small amount, this will calm them down. Then because they are calmer, they can eat more, reinforcing the calmness and, in turn, calming them down further etc. The more relaxed the dog becomes, the more they can eat, and so this continues.

Stress is automatically lowered through eating. This can be seen in humans as well! If we have had a bad day, we may reach for a chocolate bar to comfort us, and we feel calmer afterwards. Some humans take this to the extreme, which is where binge eating occurs. This is because, like dogs, we are mammals and have been conditioned to feel comforted and calmed when being nursed by our mothers. Right from the very start of life, we have been habituated to feeling soothed and relaxed during and after eating.

How Can We Help Dogs To Take Treats Outside?

There are 5 steps we can take to help a dog lower their arousal levels enough to eat comfortably when they're outside:

Step 1

Start by offering something that the dog can lick instead of them needing to chew it. Choose something like liver pate, spreadable cheese, or sandwich pastes, which can easily be licked from your hand, or a tub, for example. Even if your dog only licks it once or twice, this could be enough to reduce their arousal level slightly, which could encourage them to lick it again a few more times and so on. Once your dog is comfortable with licking, you could then offer a tasty treat that is more chewable and encourage them to eat that.

Step 2

Encourage the dog to lower their head to scavenge food from the ground. Lowering their head to sniff, search and eat treats reduces a dog's heart rate and, in turn, their arousal level too. Eating is a behaviour, and you can always train behaviour! So, in the same way you would start teaching any other new behaviour, you need to start in an area of low distraction. So, start at home, inside the house and get your dog used to actively lowering their head to eat from the ground. You can then add a cue to this, like 'seek', for example, which pairs the act of scavenging with the cue. Once this is solid, you can gradually move on to areas with higher distractions.

Step 3

Utilising ritualised tools is another great way to get a dog to perform a specific behaviour in any situation. The simplest way to use this is to teach the dog to use a snuffle mat. In the same way you would teach them to scavenge from the ground, you teach them to scavenge from the snuffle mat instead. Again, start this in training in an area with low distractions before building them up slowly. This can make it immediately apparent to the dog what they need to do as soon as they see their snuffle mat. Ritualised behaviour is often performed much more successfully in times of high stress and arousal, which is beneficial to help the dog to calm down.

Step 4

Take some tasty snacks with you on your walk, and find a quiet place where you can stop and offer some to your dog. This teaches the dog that eating and enjoying food in other locations and not only from their bowl at home is acceptable! It's helpful if you make the snacks on offer exceptionally tasty and perhaps something they would only get when they are out of the house, as this can help them look forward to them when you take a minute to stop for a snack again next time! You could use human food, too and share it with the dog, provided it's safe for them to eat.

Step 5

Using parts of the natural predatory sequence can work to your advantage! Chances are, the dog's arousal levels are heightened because they are in a hunting mood, so instead of fighting against this desire, use it to help you in a controlled way. So, if the dog is in the mood for chasing, put some food in a paper bag and get the dog interested in it by dragging it across the ground. Before you let them grab it, throw it through the air so the dog can chase it. Once they have pursued and 'caught it,' let them rip the bag open to mimic the dissection part of the predation sequence. The dog can then eat their 'kill' in the same way they would in the final part of the sequence.

Providing the dog with a replication of their natural predatory sequence means that this will naturally progress to the following stages. After they have chased, caught, killed, and eaten their prey, they would naturally experience a reduction in arousal levels which is exactly what we want to happen here!

On The Hunt For Good Behaviour

Consider this for a moment: when walking your dog, what do you do when your dog does something you like? Do you tell them 'well done', do you throw out a treat, or do you smile privately and just carry on walking?

Bearing that in mind, consider your actions when your dog does something you don't like? Do you tell them off and chastise them, do you tap their bum with your hand, call out an alternative cue, or do you ignore that behaviour completely?

The American psychologist Edward Thorndyke studied the process of learning in animals and humans. His law of effect tells us that "responses that produce a satisfying effect in a particular situation become more likely to occur again in that situation, and responses that produce a discomforting effect become less likely to occur again in that situation." In other words, attention works, but only the right kind of attention. Thorndyke believed that animals learned via trial-and-error when placed in new physical environments, so they are driven to try different behaviours to see which one 'works'.

Considering these questions, what behaviours are you inadvertently rewarding with attention, and which ones are you "punishing" by not responding to them?

When you begin to consciously give more attention to the behaviours you're encouraging, you will start to see a change in the relationship between yourself and your dog. You will be, through this conscious exercise, strengthening your bond and developing a friendship with clear communication and boundaries.

When we talk about good behaviour outdoors, this is what we look for and reinforce in your dog.

Mark and toss a treat for:

- auto check-ins: Whenever your dog looks back at you
- staying near you
- waiting instead of running off
- staying on the path
- keeping a loose leash
- etc.

Whenever your dog shows one of these behaviours, notice it actively and give them a nice treat, delivered from your hand or tossed on the ground. You will quickly see that with a little of this behaviour from you, your dog will become a lot more focused and "tuned in" on your walks.

How To Teach Your Dog To 'Check-In' with you regularly

We have previously mentioned that you should reward your dog for 'auto check-ins' but what does this actually mean, and how do you get your dog to do it?

The aim of a check-in is to teach your dog to look at you every 50 steps of your walk. This is helpful because wherever your dog is looking, this is where their attention is focused. So, if they are looking at you, they are focused on you and able to listen to any cues you need to give them. This enables you to interrupt or prevent any predatory behaviour earlier than you could if your dog never checked in with you at all.

Here is how you teach your dog to automatically check in with you:

Step 1:

Hold the long line in your hand while you walk your dog. Count the number of steps at the beginning to get a feel for when 50 steps are over and how often your dog should check in with you.

Step 2:

When your dog checks in with you (by looking at you), mark this and toss a treat on the path behind you/ into the opposite direction, so that your dog has to run past you.

If your dog hasn't checked in after 50 paces, you stop with the long line in your hand. Wait until your dog

46

gets the idea to check in with you. Now mark and throw a treat in the opposite direction.

Note:

If your dog never checks in with you, then try and really cement this game in an area with minimal distractions first. Your dog needs to first understand that checking in with you is worthwhile, and this can only be done when they are able to clearly focus on what they are being asked to do. Once they have really got the hang of it, you can increase the level of distractions around them.

You may also experience the opposite issue, where your dog constantly checks in with you and doesn't explore their environment whatsoever. In this case, only give them a food reward when you reach 50 steps. If they still check in more frequently just give them a nod, a smile, or a 'well done' without the food reward. This lets your dog know what they are doing is good, without encouraging them to check in continually in return for a food reward.

Islands Of Calmness And Islands Of Action

Dogs with high predatory energy are often over-aroused when out and about.

Predictability can be a key to calmness if your dog is very excitable outside on their walks.

It can be beneficial to create what I call "Islands of Calmness" and "Islands of Action" for your dog so that they know exactly what to expect on their walk.

An "Island of Calmness" is a place you designate or create as a sort of safe space for your dog, out in the world. It should be familiar to the senses - sight, sound, etc. - and serve as a multi-sensory cue that it's time to calm down and behave. There are several ways of creating one, and I usually suggest you start with the inside of your car. Sprinkle a few small or broken-up dog treats on the floorboards and nudge a few on the ground just outside where the car is parked. Give your dog the release cue and allow them to search for these morsels, cementing your car as a safe/good space with treats and comfort.

Choose a particular place or location on your walk and whenever you get there with your dog, take a break and let your dog calmly scan the environment for a few minutes before you move on. Sit down together on a bench or in the grass and watch the world go by.

Calmly praise your dog and stroke them in one slow but steady stroke from head to tail and from their head down to every single foot. Gentle massages and touches like these can help your dog to relax and focus on you, rather than exciting scents or darting wildlife in the environment. On your Island of Calmness, you can add in some calm activities to promote your dog's body awareness, such as slowly wading through fallen leaves or shallow water, slowly and consciously using all four feet to climb a rock, balance on a tree trunk or walking slowly and consciously across fallen branches.

Choose a different place on your walk and make it your "Island of Action." Whenever you reach this area, it's time to let your dog be a dog! Play the predation games from the Predation Substitute Games Section in this book, or any other game your dog enjoys. As the name indicates, on this island, it's time for action!

Don't forget to calm your dog down with some sprinkled treats or a "sausage tree" game before you move on, otherwise, that boundless enthusiasm might turn into frustration when the fun is over all of a sudden. (The sausage tree technique is explained in the Predation Substitute Games section later in this book.)

For the best results, your walk should always end with one last Island of Calmness before you reach the place where your car is parked, this ensures a smooth journey back home.

Extra tip:

For dogs that are very excited outside and find it hard to focus, it makes sense to walk back on the same trail, rather than walking a circular route. On the way in, they have a chance to check out the new exciting environment, while on the way back, their brain is not flooded with new information. This gives them a chance to calm down and focus on you in the second half of your journey.

Simone Mueller

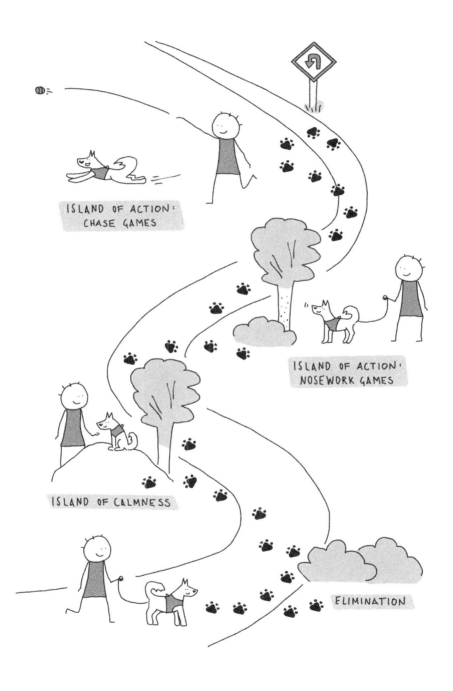

Part 2: Predation Substitute Training Tools

The Predatory Motor Pattern

Take a minute to think about your own dog. How does their body language display that they're in "hunting mode" when you are together? Do they freeze? Sniff the ground? Do they stop and stare? Or do you only become aware of your dog's intentions when they have already set off on a wild chase?

Predatory behaviour starts long before the chase begins, and it does not end with it either. Predation is a behaviour chain that actually consists of several parts - ones that are both intrinsically reinforcing for your dog and that merge into one another. Once the dog has taken the first step in that chain, he is likely to slide into the next part, and that momentum makes it very hard to interrupt them. In order to stop this progression while your dog is still approachable, we need to be able to identify predatory behaviour when it starts.

- **Orientation:** The predatory sequence starts with the dog's orientation in the environment. Is there something to huntin their immediate area? They will show orientation behaviour, such as air-scenting, scanning the environment with their eyes, or searching the area with their nose on the ground.

- **Stalking**: As soon as the dog has located possible prey, they will start to stalk the prey with their eyes. Their body language becomes tense.

- **Creeping**: Next, they will slowly and carefully creep physically forward: this gets them as close as possible to their prey before the next sequence, the chase, begins. Closing the distance on unwary prey is a natural instinct that helps ensure hunting success.

- **Chasing**: The chase is the most obvious part of the predatory sequence.

- **Grab-bite and Kill-bite**: If the dog is lucky and gets close enough to their prey, they will then grab-bite and kill-bite the prey animal, behaviours often displayed in combination with violent head shakes.

- **Possessing, Dissecting and Consuming**: After the animal is dead, the dog will often hold on to the prey animal for a while before they finally start to dissect and consume it.

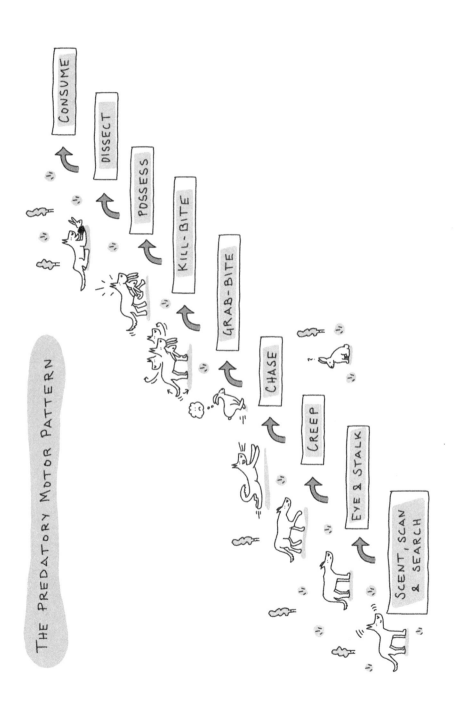

Wolves, jackals, and dingoes still have this original version of the predatory sequence in their repertoire, and an outside observer can easily watch them progress through each step of the chain. Due to artificial selection and breeding, most domestic dogs no longer perform the entire chain of behaviour reliably. Some parts have been "bred out," as humans do not typically want our dogs to display traits we consider negative for us. Other parts of the chain, however, have been highlighted as useful skills in our working dog breeds

Let's consider, for example, the predatory motor pattern displayed in a Border collie. In order to help humans with sheep herding, parts of the predatory sequence, such as eyeing/stalking, creeping, and chasing, have been highlighted through breeding and reinforcement. In contrast, the parts of the predatory chain that would signal these dogs to eat, kill, or maim the sheep they herd have been suppressed and effectively bred out.

Simone Mueller

THE PREDATORY MOTOR PATTERN OF A BORDER COLLIE

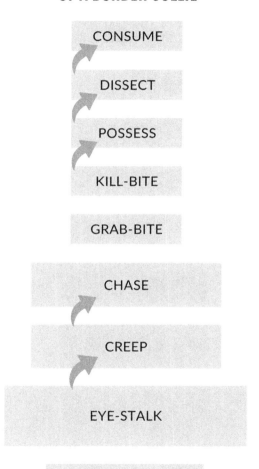

CONSUME

DISSECT

POSSESS

KILL-BITE

GRAB-BITE

CHASE

CREEP

EYE-STALK

SCENT, SCAN, SEARCH

In contrast to this selective predation chain retention, Spaniels have been selected for generations to flush game out of denser bushes. Orientating, especially searching, chasing and grab-biting have been highlighted in a Spaniel's predatory sequence. This is why their noses are almost always glued to the ground while they zig-zag the park, often oblivious to their owner's desperate recall whistles.

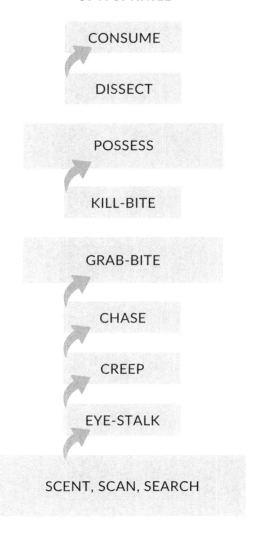

THE PREDATORY MOTOR PATTERN
OF A SPANIEL

CONSUME

DISSECT

POSSESS

KILL-BITE

GRAB-BITE

CHASE

CREEP

EYE-STALK

SCENT, SCAN, SEARCH

To illustrate a third example, a Greyhound is bred to chase. Orientating, especially with their eyes, chasing, grab-biting, and even kill-biting, has been highlighted in their breeding repertoire.

THE PREDATORY MOTOR PATTERN OF A SIGHTHOUND

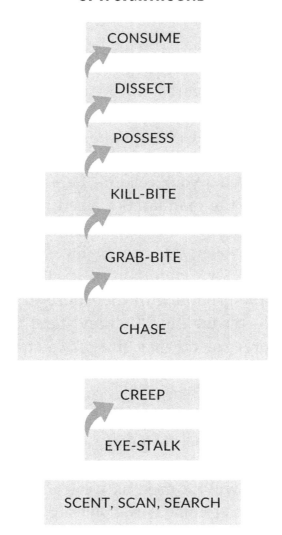

CONSUME

DISSECT

POSSESS

KILL-BITE

GRAB-BITE

CHASE

CREEP

EYE-STALK

SCENT, SCAN, SEARCH

Your Dog's Favourite Hobbies

Take a moment to consider which parts of the predatory sequence your dog may be bred to perform, and determine if any stand out. If you have a crossbreed, think of your individual dog and note down the parts that you believe they enjoy from previous observations. Also, remember that even if your dog is a purebred, they might not live up to their own breed standard: like their owners, every dog is an individual with unique likes and dislikes.

Let's pause your reading here for a moment and set down the manual. Get a pen and paper, take a long, genuine moment to think about your dog's favourite hobbies. Do they love to scan the environment for potential prey? Do they enjoy searching the ground with their nose to the floor or scenting the air up high? Do they stand and point at potential prey, or do they run off to chase straight away? Do they proudly possess and parade with a toy, or do they retrieve it directly to your hand? This may seem a little silly out of context, but this information will be absolutely crucial as we move further into the system. These thoughtful observations will be used as we learn about need-oriented games to play with your dog.

Performing Safe Parts Of The Predatory Sequence

Take a look at the predatory sequence discussed earlier and mull it over. Which parts of that chain of actions and instincts are safe for our dogs to perform in real life? Further, which ones are safe for both the dogs AND the "prey animal?"

We can sometimes allow our dog to chase after a squirrel when it's clearly already up a tree, but we should still keep in mind that this will be highly stressful for the little animal, and uncertain events can result from the commotion. Once, with my dog Nanook, I witnessed a startled squirrel fall right out of a tree and onto the ground in front of him, complete with a terrified little squirrel scream. Thankfully, my dog was so surprised at the sudden turn of events that his confusion prevented him from leaping onto the poor thing, which escaped unscathed. That doesn't mean things couldn't have gone poorly – a dog aroused by predation can manage to climb the first few branches of a tree in pursuit of prey, posing a worrisome risk of injury.

While keeping your dog out of a tree is an obviously smart precaution, knowing which components of the predatory sequence are safe can be more challenging. To clarify, there are three basic actions that your dog can be allowed to perform as a substitute for chasing, and those are the ones we'll focus on here. Thankfully, they're also the first three, which makes them easy to identify: orientation (scanning, searching and air-scenting the environment), stalking a trigger and creeping towards that trigger.

Orientation, stalking and creeping are the parts of the predatory sequence that we can let our dogs perform in real-life situations. Careful training can change our dog's initial reaction when they encounter wildlife. Instead of chasing wildlife and putting the "prey animal" and themselves in danger, we can teach them to stand and stalk. That way, they still perform parts of the predatory sequence and have a real predatory experience that fulfils their canine needs, but they do it in a safe way.

We cannot, of course, ever allow our dogs to grab and kill wildlife - that is an absolute no-go! As part of that effort, we know that we can never allow our dogs to possess, dissect or consume animals they have killed.

Our dogs, however, still have the need to perform all the parts of the predatory sequence. They don't know that we live in a world where certain parts of the predatory motor pattern are not acceptable. To come as close to the real experience as possible, we play Predation Substitute Games. But don't fool yourself! Our dogs know that a game is just a game and not the real thing. Yet, it's at least something!

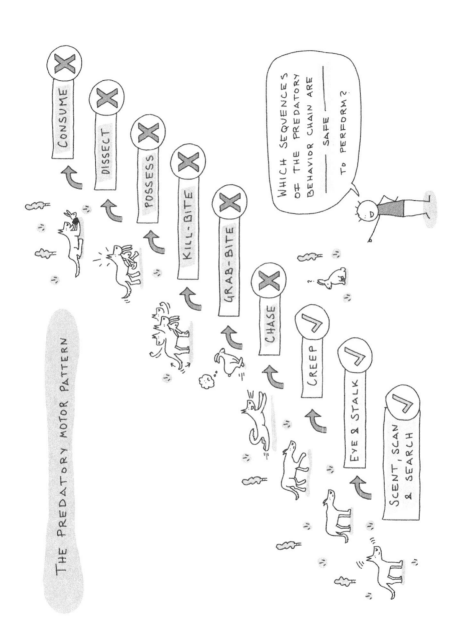

The Real Stuff And The Sugar-Free Version – A Metaphor

What's the difference between Predation Substitute Tools and Predation Substitute Games?

Let me give you an example from our human world: Everybody knows excessive sugar consumption is not good for you. I love drinking Coke and would like to drink Coke every single day. Of course, this wouldn't be healthy, as Coke contains a lot of sugar. So I can't have a real Coke every day, but I can at least have a diet Coke. After I had it, I don't feel thirsty anymore. I have enjoyed the nice taste that comes close to the original taste. So for me, having a sugar-free Coke is better than having no Coke at all.

The predatory motor pattern is the sugary Coke. It can be harmful to our dogs. Predation Substitute Games, such as Backtracking or the Sausage Tree, are the sugar-free versions. We offer our dogs a safe way to fulfill their needs by playing "sugar-free" Predation Substitute Games to make up for the unsafe parts of the predatory sequence that they can't perform in real life.

We can play Predation Substitute Games daily and as much as our dogs want. From time to time, however, we come across opportunities to give our dogs a healthy ration of the real stuff. This is where Predation Substitute Tools, such as scanning, air-scenting or stalking on cue, come into play.

Let's talk about this "real stuff", the Predation Substitute Tools: Although an excessive sugar consumption is bad for you, a little bit of sugar won't do any harm. Let's say the predatory sequence from the very first part of orientation in the environment to the very last part of consuming prey equals a whole bottle of Coke.

Drinking a whole bottle of Coke is not healthy, however, every now and then, it's ok to have a glass of real Coke. By using the Predation Substitute Tools, which are the safe parts of the predatory sequence, in a real-life context, our dogs can have a glass of real coke every now and then. Having the real stuff tastes much better, and just like us, our dogs can tell the difference between real-life predation and "the sugar-free" version.

Reinforcing The Three Safe Parts Of The Predatory Motor Pattern

Scanning The Environment

Scanning in the context of our training means the action of your dog standing and scanning the environment around them, looking for potential prey.

Dogs often show this behaviour when coming out of woodland into an open field or when reaching the top of a hill – essentially, when their visual environment changes in a dramatic way. Orientation for prey is the very first stage of the predatory behaviour chain, so often, the level of arousal is still relatively low. Your dog is asking themself: "Is there potential prey in my environment or not?" This means that there does not necessarily need to be a traditional trigger. Be aware, however, that arousal can increase rapidly if your dog finds out that there is indeed prey nearby.

Watch your dog to see if they are performing a visual scan (they will be actively looking around, NOT completely focused on one trigger), air scenting (they will lift their nose into the air and their nostrils will twitch) or listening to noises that might tell them that prey is around (their ears will be pointed forward or twitching sideways)

As humans, we are not always 100% sure which "channel" our dog is tuned into at any given moment. Maybe they are seeing something, maybe they are scenting something, maybe both simultaneously. This is why we don't need to differentiate these behaviours. We can use one single cue: "Scan".

The Protocol:

- When your dog stops in order to scan the environment with sight, smell, or sound for potential prey, you stop as well. Calmly praise your dog and repeat the cue as long as they are showing the behaviour: "Good boy/girl – scan – good boy/girl – scan ..."
- When your dog is ready to move on, move on with them. No treat needed.
- If your dog gets very aroused, you might be too close to potential prey. Try to interrupt the behaviour with a positive interrupter, such as a hand touch and increase the distance between you and the potential prey. You can either try again from a distance or play a Predation Substitute Game to release their energy.

Nanook scanning on cue.

Orientation within the environment is not only need-oriented; many dogs naturally love to do it. So, take a break on your walks, sit down on a bench or even in the grass together with your dog and scan the environment for a while. Your dog will be mentally stimulated, taking in and processing all the various visual, olfactory, and auditory information. They will be satisfied and tired after you come home, but in a calmer and more relaxed way: this behaviour is both enriching and fulfilling to them!

Searching The Environment

Searching in the context of our training refers to your dog using their nose down on the ground and actively sniffing for the scent(s) of potential prey.

The Protocol:

- To put searching on cue, scatter some treats and send your dog to search in that area. While their nose is down on the ground, sniffing, capture the behaviour by calmly repeating the cue "search – search – search..." several times.
- You can prompt the behaviour by pointing your index finger to the ground where the scattered treats are and making a stirring movement. By stirring and not pointing, you narrow down the search area for your dog without spoiling the fun by helping too much.

Special Tip:

The next time you practice your recall together, scatter some treats next to you before you call your dog and send them into the search with your "stirring finger" as soon as they arrive.

Simone Mueller

Isla searching on cue.

Stalking A Trigger

Stalking, in the context of our training, consists of your dog standing and watching a nearby trigger, such as a deer, squirrel, or rabbit.

The important concept we're teaching them here is: You cannot chase, but you can stand and watch that trigger as long as you want to!

Remember: a dog that is standing is not chasing! This sounds super simple, but bear in mind that standing instead of running off is a super effective and clever alternative behaviour.

By training your dog according to their innate needs, and positively reinforcing the behaviour of standing and watching the trigger, this safe part of the predatory sequence gets reinforced. Your dog will show the behaviour more often and for longer periods of time in the future. That extra time gives you more space to react: putting your dog on a lead, asking for a recall, or offering a game to divert that urge to chase.

If you come across a deer, for example, your dog will not chase it immediately, but they will stand and watch it a little longer than they might do with something else. That's because this alternative behaviour serves a function: they are still indulging in the hunt; they simply haven't moved through the progression of the chain yet. They're receiving the chemical rewards in their brain for performing an instinctive behaviour, and this careful balance keeps them satisfied and safe at your side.

Rather than completely interrupting and ending the predatory sequence, allow your dog to stay within it. Performing the intrinsically reinforcing parts of the predatory behaviour chain feels very good to them!

A Note On Safety:

For safety's sake, do NOT allow your dog to stalk children or other pets, especially smaller dogs! Your dog can sometimes get carried away by the emotions and hormones that are released into their body during the predatory sequence. They then might mistake a child or another dog for prey and attempt to grab or even kill it. This phenomenon is called predatory drift, and it can be life-threatening, especially to smaller children and pets.

Additionally, another dog may perceive the tense, arrow-shaped body posture of a stalking dog as a threat, and might feel compelled to act aggressively against your dog in defense. If you notice your dog stalking a child or another pet, immediately ask for a check-in from them or recall them as soon as you notice. This helps keep both your pet and others in their environment safe and secure.

Stage 1 – Establishing A Solid Stalk

In order to put your dog's stalking behaviour on cue, you'll need to capture it when your dog is showing it naturally. For example, if your dog is standing and watching a deer at a distance where they are still calm and approachable, then quietly name the behaviour with the cue "see it". Assigning the cue a particular phrase will help bolster your communication with your dog, and will also help you control and trigger the behaviour proactively in later training sessions.

The Protocol:

- If you have noticed a wild animal, but your dog hasn't yet, put them on a lead and approach the trigger in a curve. It's vital that you stay behind your dog and follow their lead.
- As soon as your dog sees the trigger and stops, stop as well. Do not lead them any closer! If your dog is about to get too close to the trigger without seeing it or if your dog increases speed (preclude to a chase), gently slow your dog down into a stop.
- While calmly watching the wild animal, it doesn't matter if your dog is sitting, lying or standing, as long as they have four feet on the ground. Make sure the leash is slack, and they can stand on their own.
- Start praising your dog in a calm voice as long as they are stalking the trigger and repeat the verbal cue several times: "Good boy/girl – see it – good boy/girl – see it ..." Do this as long as your dog chooses to stalk. Remember, the deal here is that you're telling them: You cannot chase, but you can watch as long as you want to!
- When your dog checks in with you, calmly ask them whether they want to stalk again. If they don't, the two of you walk on.

- If your dog turns around and is super excited, reward them AWAY from the trigger with a high-value treat or toy.

Basic Rules:

- Always make sure that the lead is slack and your dog can stand on their own without you holding them back. In order to work off-leash later on, there should be no pressure applied to the lead at this stage.
- Dogs that love to stalk often choose to stalk as a reinforcement, rather than opting for a treat. So let them keep stalking!
- Dogs that are very excited and want to chase should be rewarded with a substitute "sugar-free" chase AWAY from the trigger! Toss a high-value treat or throw a toy in another direction once you've put enough distance between the two of you and the trigger.
- Be careful not to reward your dog for checking in with you all the time! You do not want to accidentally establish an interrupter or check-in cue. You want the stalk to continue.
- Do not name the behaviour when your dog is already over threshold and giving chase! In classical conditioning, you always condition the emotion that the dog is feeling together with the cue. If you name the stalk while your dog is already super aroused and barking and lunging, he will never be able to stand and stalk calmly when he hears this cue again in the future.

- If your dog is already over the chase threshold, call your dog away by using a recall or a hand touch that will be described in the last section of the book, increase the distance between the pair of you and the trigger until you reach a distance from which your dog can calmly stand and watch the trigger. Now try again.
- Standing and watching calmly costs a lot of impulse control. Do not overtrain your dog! A short session of three minutes is enough. Additionally, do not attempt to train this protocol when you or your dog have had a bad day. If your dog met their canine nemesis in the park earlier on this walk, they will already be too upset to be able to perform a nice, calm stalk. Trigger stacking is something we always want to avoid.

Important!

Don't underestimate the distance that your dog may need to not go over threshold while standing calmly and watching the trigger! At the beginning of your training journey, you might need to stay several hundred meters away. This is totally dependent on your dog and how strong their predatory motivation is. This exercise is NOT about physically stalking wildlife and getting closer and closer! It's all about a visual stalk, standing calmly and enjoying the experience.

Simone Mueller

Nanook stalking on cue.

This is what it looks like.

Troubleshooting

How do I know that my dog is under threshold?

•Dogs are only able to learn, when they are under threshold.

There are two good indicators: Firstly, your dog is calmly standing, four feet on the ground, and secondly, they can stand on their own, which means their leash is slack.

My dog does not look at the trigger, they always look at me:

- Take your time, breathe in and out slowly, and relax your whole body so that even your hand that is holding the leash is not tense anymore.
- Put away all the treats and the toys so that your dog is not distracted by them.
- Do not put your hand into your treat bag before your dog shows the behaviour that you want to have. Avoid noisy, rustling treat bags in your pocket also.
- Most importantly, do not look back at your dog! Look at the "prey" instead. Eventually, your dog will turn around and follow your gaze to see what you are looking at - this is the moment you calmly start to cue and praise: "Good boy/girl – see it – good boy/girl – see it ..."

My dog looks at the trigger, but then they check in with me all the time:

- Check yourself for the points mentioned above.
- As soon as your dog looks at the "prey," start to praise them in a low, calm voice. Repeat the cue several times, like a mantra.
- If your dog turns around to look at you, immediately stop talking.
- Look at the trigger and wait. The second they turn towards the "prey" again, start to praise and cue again. Remember, stalking is a self-reinforcing behaviour, but, if you feel the need to give them a treat, do so while your dog is still in position, actively looking at the "prey"

How do I know when I need to reward my dog AWAY from the trigger and when I can simply praise them calmly and move on after he disengaged from the "prey"?

- To be honest, this is the hardest part of this type of training. It all comes down to reading your dog and their body language and feeling what they need at this moment.
- Option 1: Your dog is calm while they are stalking the "prey" and able to disengage quite easily, their body language is quite relaxed, and they are still able to show cut off signals, such as blinking, twitching an ear or flicking their tongue. As long as they're showing these signs, then you can praise them calmly and ask

them to go for a sniff or see whether they want to stalk again.

- Option 2: If your dog's body language is tense, the surface of their body is completely frozen and their centre of gravity is pointed towards the trigger like an arrow, they are on the verge of sliding into the next part of the predatory sequence: The chase. If your dog is now still able to disengage from the "prey" and check-in with you instead of chasing off towards the prey, they deserve lots of praise: this is an amazing achievement! Remember what we've already covered on functional and need-oriented rewards and give them what they need: a substitute, "sugar-free" version of a chase. Throw a high-value treat or toy AWAY from the trigger. Give them enthusiastic verbal praise. Give them some time to possess the prey and carry it around. Then, allow them to eat from the toy or out of the prey dummy and scatter some treats to calm them down again. Try to mimic the curve of arousal that we learned about earlier in this training manual.

My dog is still stalking the trigger, but I need to move on:

- In general, allow your dog to look at the trigger as long as they wish to do so.
- If you. for some reason, need to move on, step sideways into your dog's peripheral vision, move your hand and address your dog with their name or make a kissy noise. When they

turn towards you, mark and move backwards into the direction away from the trigger. Reward with a treat or toy further AWAY from the trigger.

- If your dog still does not react, give them a little tap on their backend, no harder than if you were tapping someone's shoulder - this is not a spank or punishment, it just gets your dog's attention. As soon as they react, mark and move backwards while you make a kissy noise. Reward with a toy or treat AWAY from the trigger.

Beware of redirected aggression if your dog is not used to being tapped. They might be so focused on the "prey" that they completely forget everything around them. If you are not sure about this, condition the tap with treats at home first before putting it into action outside.

The protocol here is: Tap – treat – tap –treat – tap – treat – tap ... wait: Does your dog expect a treat?

If Yes: You have now created a positive emotional response in your dog after being tapped, and you can use this tactic out in the world with them.
If No: Repeat the tapping and treating until your dog expects a treat.

My dog is stalking intensely, and I am afraid that they will be going over threshold in a few moments.

- Going over threshold is something that should not happen often, so as to avoid linking high arousal with the act of stalking. It will, however, inevitably happen from time to time. As your dog is in their seeking system during predation, going over a threshold here is not as severe a concern as going over threshold in a fear-related situation. The dog will most likely not suffer any long-term damage from it.
- When you are afraid that your dog will go over threshold, apply the same methods described above for when you need to move on: Step sideways into your dog's peripheral vision, move your hand and address your dog with their name or make a kissy noise. When they turn towards you, mark and move backwards into the direction away from the trigger. Reward with a treat or toy further AWAY from the trigger.
- If your dog still does not react, give them a little tap on their backend, no harder than if you were tapping someone's shoulder - this is not a spank or punishment, it just gets their attention. As soon as they react, mark and move backwards while you make a kissy noise. Reward with a toy or treat AWAY from the trigger.
- Put some distance between you and the trigger until you reach the point where your dog can calmly stand and watch. Now try again - it's a

process, but it's ultimately a rewarding one for both of you.

My dog is barking and lunging and is not able to stalk the trigger calmly with four feet on the ground.

- You are likely too close to the trigger. Your dog is not able to learn as long as they are over threshold. Use the "emergency exit" covered later in this book to remove your dog and try again from a much greater distance.
- If they have gone completely over threshold and aren't responding to all these measures, grab their harness as a last resort and guide them out of the situation.

Once your dog is proficient in and able to perform a nice long stalk without constantly checking in with you, then you are ready for Stage 2.

Stalking Stage 2: Asking for an Alternative Behaviour

Once your dog has learned what the cue "see it" means and can show nice long stalks in various contexts and environments, you are now ready to ask them to perform an alternative behaviour while they are stalking.

The alternative behaviour should be incompatible with the unwanted behaviour of chasing and it should be something that the dog likes to do, that is easy to perform and that has a solid reinforcement history, which means that it has been heavily reinforced and generalized in the past.

In my own training, I use a "sit" here. A sit has various advantages: The dog can perform it while he is stalking, without interrupting the stalk. For most dogs, sitting is very easy, as it has been practised and rewarded a great deal previously, and may have even been the first cue they ever learned.

Why put an alternative behaviour between the stalk and the marker?

This serves three functions:

1. It makes the position of the dog more stable. Most dogs are more likely to run off while in a stand. The sit, conversely, has often already been trained in combination with a sit-stay. For a dog with this type of training, it is quite clear that they are supposed to stay where they are.
2. Performing a learned behaviour activates the thinking part of the brain. During the stalk, the dog is very likely to switch to a primitive part of the brain that handles emotions and instincts. By letting them perform a learned behaviour, we bring them back from their own dog world into our human world, making them more approachable for us and less likely to run off.
3. Checking your dog's threshold. ASK your dog to perform the alternative behaviour. It is not a command. It is a question: "Fido, can you sit?"

By asking whether your dog can sit or not, you can check their level of arousal. If they are not able to sit or you need to ask them several times before they can perform, they might be at threshold with a higher risk of chasing. Try to interrupt the stalk with the help of a positive interrupter such as a hand touch. Step sideways into your dog's peripheral vision, move your hand and address your dog with their name or make a kissy noise. When they turn towards you, mark and move backwards into the direction away from the trigger. Reward with a treat or toy further AWAY from the trigger.

If your dog still does not react, give them a little tap on their backend to get their attention. As soon as they react, mark and move backwards while you make a kissy noise. Reward with a toy or treat AWAY from the trigger.

Increase distance until your dog is able to calmly watch the "prey" with four feet on the ground, and start the stalk again.

Stalking Stage 2: The Protocol
- As before, approach the trigger in a curve. Stay behind your dog and follow.
- As soon as your dog sees the trigger and stops, you stop too. If your dog is about to get too close to the trigger without seeing it, gently slow your dog down into a halt.
- Make sure the leash is slack and they can stand on their own.

- Start praising your dog in a calm voice as long as they are stalking the trigger and repeat the cue "Good boy/girl – see it – good boy/girl – see it ..."
- Then, ask for the alternative behaviour: "Fido, can you sit?"
- Your dog sits and continues to stalk, praise them again: "Good boy/girl – see it – good boy/girl – see it ..."
- If they are not able to sit, ask again. If they're still not able to sit, interrupt the stalk with a positive interrupter, such as a hand touch, increase distance, until your dog is able to calmly watch the "prey" with four feet on the ground, and try again.

Isla stalking on cue plus alternative behaviour: SITTING.

Capturing The First Steps Of The Indication Of Wildlife

The problem with working with predation is that you can't control the environment as much as you can when you are working with other behaviours. After all, you cannot ask a deer to turn up at 3pm for your walk so you can practice your dog's training!

However, what you can do is go to areas where you know that your dog is likely to be able to be successful. For example, if you know that there are usually cows in a field nearby, you can use this as a training opportunity. Generally, cows are quite still, they don't tend to charge around very often or make much noise, so they can be a good place to start. Make sure your dog is at a large enough distance away from the cows that they are still in a thinking state so they can still and listen to your cues. Allow them to quietly and calmly watch the cows and reward them for doing so. This is the start of teaching your dog that standing and stalking wildlife is a good option, which pays off for them. Most dogs are unaware of this, instead choosing to immediately chase any wildlife they see. So, it's up to us to teach them that calmly stalking is more preferable than mindless chasing.

To set your dog up for success, don't wait until you actually come across wildlife that you can't control.

Instead, try to train FOR the situation by capturing tiny indications of wildlife and hereby laying a solid reinforcement history before moving on to wildlife that is visible to the dog.

Here's how you can teach your dog to calmly indicate wildlife:

Walk behind your dog and whenever they THINK that there is wildlife in the bushes and stop for a second, you stop too and start to cue and praise "See it – good see it etc." for as long as the dog stands and stalks.

Your dog will soon realise that there is nothing there, but if they check in with you now, mark and throw a treat into the OPPOSITE direction.

Extra Tip:

You can even trigger an initial indication by throwing a stone into the bushes. Always try to capture your dog standing and staring. It's best to keep your dog on a long line so that they don't run off or try and chase.

Part 3 Hunting Together! – Creating An Outlet Through Predation Substitute Games

We cannot allow our dogs to chase, grab, or kill a living animal - no matter how natural the behaviour may come to them. It's inhumane and an absolute no-go! However, our dogs still have these innate needs, and instead of trying to completely suppress them, we can at least give them the "sugar-free" version of the real stuff. That's why, as responsible dog owners, we play games that mimic parts of the predatory sequence in order to give our dogs an outlet for their predatory energy.

These are all easy games that you can play on your walks, or they can be used as functional reinforcers after a successful recall, a reward for not chasing a trigger, and so on.

Let Your Dog Be A Dog!

Before we get into the games, there are a few things that need to be said: these games are NOT about impulse control. They are NOT about interrupting the fun by asking your dog to perform a learned behaviour before allowing them to play the game as a "treat." In other words, training takes place in part 1 and part 3 of this book, and this is the chapter where the fun happens.

In each of the following games, allow your dog to follow their impulses, and instincts and to act out their innate needs. These games are, at their core, all about letting your dog be a dog.

This is why you should only ask your dog to perform a sit-stay if they are capable of doing it without you having to correct them while you prepare the games. If your dog is not able to hold themselves back, ask a helper to hold their lead for you or tie the leash around a tree while your dog has to wait; don't rely on them to self-regulate when these games are designed to get them worked up a bit.

Equipment

To play Predation Substitute Games, you will need many high-value treats. The treats should be flavourful, soft, and easy to chew, such as cooked liver, cut cheese, or hot dogs.

You will also need a toy that your dog loves! You can use any dog toy, but I highly recommend the use of a so-called lotus ball, snack dummy or prey dummy.

A prey dummy is a toy originally developed for gun dog training. It looks like a pencil case with a zipper and can be stuffed with treats. Some prey dummies even have rabbit fur, sheepskin, or fake fur on the outside for further enticement. The perks of these prey dummies are that parts of the predatory sequence, such as grabbing and possessing, feel much more authentic to the dog when there's fur present to bite into. It's so authentic, in fact, that some dogs even start to dissect the fur straight away.

You can also feed your dog out of the prey dummy or lotus ball, which means it will satisfy the final part of the predatory sequence: consuming the prey. This will, in turn, lead to the release of endorphins that will calm your dog down. Do not simply give your dog a treat out of the prey dummy, let them stick their nose into the prey dummy and enjoy the feeling of consuming their prey – this is where the satisfaction and that valuable "cooling down" come from.

Another positive aspect of using a prey dummy is that only you can open the zipper or velcro and give your dog access to the treats inside. Successful hunting is teamwork! Your dog will learn that it is beneficial to share their prey with you.

You will also need a three to five-meter leash or a ten-metre long line, attached to a well-fitted harness. Retractable leads and leads that are shorter than two meters are not suitable for these need-oriented games, as they do not offer enough play and manoeuvrability.

Equipment

The Curve Of Arousal

When a dog is in "hunting mode", a cocktail of hormones is released into their body that strongly influences their behaviour and level of arousal. By the time your dog is ready to grab and kill-bite a prey animal, their body is already full of adrenaline and dopamine. Their pain perception is reduced, and their focus is narrowed down to the object of the hunt. This is an extremely powerful motivating factor for them: imagine what it takes to face down a wild boar or an impressive stag in the wild and decide to attack it! When chasing an animal, your dog might not even physically be able to hear your attempts to recall: the "thinking" part of their canine brain has already been rerouted. They have engaged a primal part of their brain, and until the hunt is over, diverted, or interrupted, it will be responsible for their basic emotions and instinctive behaviour.

Even after the kill, it takes a while for these potent hormones to ebb. That's why your dog will still hold on to the prey for a while before they start to dissect and consume it. When that happens, endorphins are released, and you'll notice your dog calms down. Like all mammals, the act of chewing and licking has a naturally soothing effect on them, as it is associated with feeding and rest.

You can actively relax your dog after a wild chasing game or a tug-o-war by consciously activating the low-arousal-level parts of the predatory sequence to release endorphins. This tactic reduces the frustration that inevitably sets in when the game abruptly stops at its climax. Think of this technique as being the canine equivalent of a "cool down" after a heavy workout at the gym or strenuous exercise. In other words, you're still moving, the endorphins are still flowing, but you aren't going full speed at your original goal any longer.

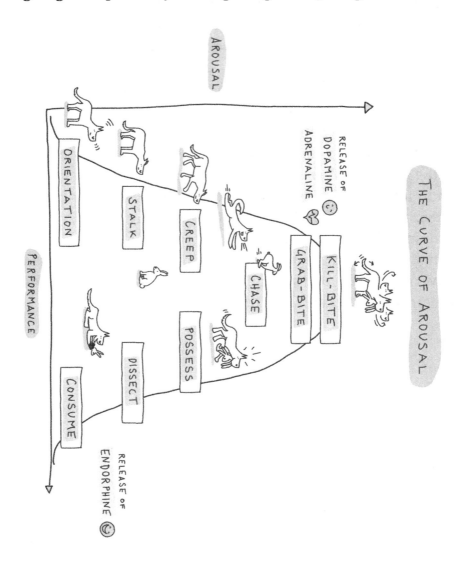

Dog parks are full of well-meaning owners that throw a ball around for 20 minutes with their dog, return home with them, and then expect the dog to sleep while they are off to work. The problem is that the dog has been repeating the two most arousing parts of the predatory motor pattern over and over: chase and grab-bite. Now, they're left home alone, still pumped full of adrenaline and dopamine. They need a cool down to ease the frustration and to soothe themselves, so they may rip apart the couch or chew the carpet, as those are the only coping tools they have at their disposal.

It's important to note here that I'm not implying there's anything wrong with engaging in play with your dog! You do not need to avoid high-arousal play, on the contrary, it's important for our dogs to blow off steam and to work physically. That being said, it's important not to leave your dog ramped up, frustrated, and stuck in a super-excited state. Cool them down by letting them hold on to their "prey," and do not expect them to retrieve and give the toy to you straight away. Rather, admire and praise them actively for what they have in their grip, and encourage them to carry around their prey. When they settle and put the toy down, do not immediately grab the toy, particularly if you're attempting to wind down from a play session. Take some treats and put them onto the toy, so that your dog can eat the treats from the toy, while calmly praising them for being such a good dog. Then, sprinkle even more treats around the toy, and gradually away from the toy to divert their energy into the "eating" and cool-down stage of the hunt. Only then take the toy and put it away into your pocket or out of your dog's sight/reach.

On your way home and throughout the house, sprinkle some more treats into the grass and on the floor.

Scavenging and searching for food is excellent for lowering your dog's level of arousal and excitement naturally. Before you leave the house to work, give your dog a stuffed Kong toy or a Lickimat to soothe themselves while you are gone: again, this reinforces the "cool down" mindset and allows them to wind down naturally.

The Free Search

A need-oriented game for dogs that like to search

In this game, you will send your dog to search an area with their nose in order to find a hidden toy or prey dummy.

Free Search: The Protocol

Free Search Step 1

Ask a helper to hold your dog or tie the leash around a tree. "Hide" the toy or prey dummy where your dog can see it. Send your dog to search for the prey dummy. As soon as your dog finds it, it's party time!

Remember: It's all about having fun and letting your dog be a dog! After they find their hidden prize, do not ask your dog to retrieve the prey dummy or let go of it. Whatever behaviour your dog offers is worth praise and admiration. If your dog wants to possess the toy and run around with it, praise them for doing it. They are performing parts of the predatory sequence, not playing a controlled game of fetch-and-retrieve with you.

If your dog chooses to lie down with it and nibble the fur, ask if they would like you to open the prey dummy for them, so they can eat out of it. Put some treats on the prey dummy or toy and let your dog eat from the toy to further calm them down. Eventually, work up to scattering some treats away from the toy. Once your dog is engaged in hunting down those treats, place the toy away in a pocket or bag, out of their sight.

Free Search Step 2

Hide the toy or prey dummy out of sight in high grass, behind a rock or a trunk, or hang it on bushes or branches. You can even loosely cover it with sand or fallen leaves for a greater challenge. Send your dog to search for the prey dummy and give them lots of verbal praise when they find it. Follow the protocol from step 1 to calm your dog down and remove the prey dummy.

Free Search Step 3

Hide the toy or prey dummy in a challenging place, one that your dog cannot immediately see. Don't send your dog to search for it straight away, but instead pretend to hide the dummy in several other places. This will give them several places to look, extending the excitement and rewarding feeling they'll experience as they search the whole area.

Nanook playing Free Search.

The Stalking Game

A need-oriented game for dogs that like to stalk

In this game, your dog learns to stay with four feet on the ground and only "chase" a moving treat or toy only with their eyes.

The Stalking Game – The Protocol

Your dog is sitting or standing next to you or in front of you. Let your dog know that the game is about to start by giving them the verbal cue "See it" that was discussed earlier in the book in the chapter about stalking on cue. Wait a moment for them to process, and then slowly move a treat in front of your dog's eyes, just for a short moment. Ensure they have all four feet on the ground and their eyes on the treat, then mark and throw the treat in the direction of your last move, allowing your dog to jump after the treat.

The goal for this game is that your dog learns to stop and patiently follow the treat with their eyes. Once they show proficiency, you can let them stalk longer, or even vary your hand movements: sometimes quickly and in a zig-zag, sometimes slowly and in a curve. Try to imitate the movements of a mouse or a rabbit. Slowly increase distractions as you practice the game together.

Isla playing the stalking game.

Troubleshooting

My dog does not look at the treat but at me.
- You may need to hold your hand closer to your dog's eyes.

My dog is jumping towards the treat.
- Do not hold your hand in front of your dog's snout, but above their head, forcing them to look with their eyes, rather than follow the treat with their muzzle or mouth.

Backtracking

A need-oriented game for dogs that like to chase, grab and possess

In this game, you'll send your dog to chase along a path, following your track to a lost toy or prey dummy on the way.

Backtracking: The Protocol

Backtracking: Step 1

Bring your dog to stand next to you on a path or forest road. Let your dog watch as you drop a toy or prey dummy behind you. Prompt your dog to look behind you and send your dog to get it with the cue "Lost". As soon as your dog reaches the prey dummy, it's party time!

Remember: It's all about having fun and letting your dog be a dog! After they find the "lost" prize, do not ask your dog to retrieve the prey dummy or let go of it. Whatever behaviour your dog offers is worth praise and admiration. If your dog wants to possess the toy and run around with it, praise them for doing it. They are performing parts of the predatory sequence, not playing a controlled game of fetch-and-retrieve with you.

If your dog chooses to lie down with it and nibble the fur, ask if they would like you to open the prey dummy for them, so they can eat out of it. Put some treats on the prey dummy or toy and let your dog eat from the toy to further calm them down. Eventually, work up to scattering some treats away from the toy. Once your dog is engaged in hunting down those treats, place the toy away in a pocket or bag, out of their sight.

Backtracking Step 2

Drop your prey dummy without your dog noticing or calling attention to it the way you did in step 1. Walk a few steps forward and call your dog. Prompt behind you and send your dog to get the prey dummy with the cue "Lost." Celebrate with lots of verbal praise when your dog reaches the dummy. Admire whatever your dog does with the toy, and in the end, feed them out of the prey dummy.

Backtracking Step 3

Gradually increase the distance between your drop and when you give the "Lost" cue. Add in curves, turns and transitions between different surfaces to keep them engaged. Reduce/minimize your prompts, encouraging them to problem-solve the hunt.

Nanook playing Backtracking.

Basic Rules:

- Always drop the toy ON the track! Do not hide it. This particular Predation Substitute Game is about seeing and chasing prey, not about searching.
- If your dog starts to search instead of chase, the step-up in criteria was too hard, scale it back.
- Your dog does not have to retrieve the toy and give it back to you if they don't want to! If they want to possess the prey dummy, admire them for what they have in their mouth. Possessing is a part of the predatory sequence too, and your dog should be allowed to perform it.

The Chase Game

A need-oriented game for dogs that like to chase and grab

For the Chase Game, you will need some larger treats or little meatballs. This game is about chasing a visual trigger, so the treats should be large enough for your dog to spot them when being tossed.

The Chase Game – The Protocol

- Toss your dog a freebie treat underhand. Your movement should look like you are bowling.
- Wait for your dog to find and eat the treat. The moment your dog turns around to ask for more, mark and throw another treat energetically in the opposite direction. Repeat several times. Bowl the treats back and forth until your dog has chased enough.
- Do not forget to follow the curve of arousal and cool down your dog by gradually reducing the dynamic of the flying treat. Toss treats more gently and closer to you until you finally hand your dog some treats directly, scattering some more on the ground nearby for them to graze at.

Isla playing the Chasing Game.

Killing The Paper Bag

A need-oriented game for dogs that like to grab and dissect

In this game, your dog will be "killing", i.e. grabbing and dissecting a paper bag". It's a variation of both the Free Search and Backtracking games. Instead of using a toy or prey dummy, you use something that your dog can rip apart after they find it.

Take a paper bag, sandwich paper, wrapping paper, a toilet roll or a small carton box and stuff it with yummy treats. Rather than hiding or "losing" a toy, use the stuffed paper bag to play the Predation Substitute Games Free Search and Backtracking. Once your dog has found your manufactured prey, they can then shred it and eat the treats inside, just as they would with natural prey.

Dogs love the sound and the sensation of ripping paper or cloth because dissecting and consuming prey is a satisfying part of the predatory sequence. If you find that your dog is baffled by the paper bag or box initially, help them by ripping the paper together, and encourage them to indulge in that feeling together with you.

Special Tip: Take a treat-stuffed toilet roll on your walk and throw it as a surprise reward after a rapid recall. Your dog will learn positive associations with the concept and look forward to playing games that use a similar "prey" in the future.

Nanook playing Killing the Paper Bag.

The Sausage Tree

A need-oriented game for dogs that like to search, consume and scavenge

The Sausage Tree is an extremely simple game, but it ambitiously covers the very first and the very last part of the predatory sequence: searching and consuming. Both are connected with a low level of arousal, making this game an excellent choice for "cooling down" periods.

In searching and consuming, the predatory sequence comes to a full circle. After a high arousal chase, dopamine is finally released and calms down your dog's system. The hunt has come to an end, and your dog is satiated and easier to control now that he has completed this incredibly important part of the predatory sequence. Through this game, they will feel calm, relaxed, and satisfied in their instinctive brain.

Feral dogs spend hours every day scavenging. The behaviour not only gives their day structure and purpose, but it also provides the nourishment they need to survive. To mimic and encourage this behaviour in your domesticated dog, throw a handful of treats into the grass, sprinkle treats into fallen leaves or pin pieces of cheese or sausage onto the lowest twigs and branches of a tree or bush your dog can reach before sending your dog to find them. The Sausage Tree should be used to mark the end of every training session on predation.

Simone Mueller

Isla playing the Sausage Tree.

Functional, Need-Oriented Reinforcers

Like humans, every dog has innate needs. To fulfil these needs, dogs follow certain behaviours. If the results of this behaviour meet those innate needs, then we say that the behaviour is functional. Understanding that performing X action will lead to Y fulfilment, the dog will instinctively perform it in the future to have their needs fulfilled. If the behaviour is not functional and does not fulfil their needs, they will logically reduce or eliminate this behaviour: dogs are creatures of efficiency where their needs are concerned.

When your dog sees a deer, their motivation is to chase the deer. If you recall your dog, he might turn away from the deer and run to you instead. When this happens, you might offer them a dry biscuit - but that still doesn't meet their innate needs - even though it's edible, the biscuit isn't "prey," so the parts that are telling them to chase-bite-kill are still riled up and ready to go. Therefore the behaviour of following your recall and returning to you is not functional. That means that they will reduce this behaviour in the future, and may even ignore your recall next time.

Even if you offered them super yummy chicken instead of a dry biscuit, this is still not a functional reward. Yes, again, it is edible and of higher quality than the biscuit, but what your dog is really looking to do in the scenario is to go for a hunt: chase, bite, kill and only then eat.

This is the reason why our recall so often goes unheard, even if we reinforce our cues with super yummy treats that our dog loves. Eating is not a functional, need-oriented reward in a situation when our dog wants to chase: necessary for survival, yes, but that little canine voice in their head that wants to chase-bite-kill in a hunt is going unanswered entirely.

Functional, need-oriented reinforcers are super strong rewards, as they actually provide your dog with what they need to do or have to bring that predatory energy to a natural end in your play session or outing.

Have another look at the list of your dog's favourite hobbies and think of functional, need-oriented rewards that you can give to your dog. What can you offer them that mimics the parts of the predatory sequence that your dog in particular loves to perform?

Some Examples Of Functional And Need-Oriented Reinforcers:

Functional reinforcers for dogs that like to scan, scent and search:

- Using Predation Substitute Tools such as Air-Scenting, Scanning on Cue
- Playing Predation Substitute Games such as Treat Scattering in the grass
- Playing the Free Search using a prey dummy
- Playing the Sausage Tree game

Functional reinforcers for dogs that like to eye and stalk:

- Using Predation Substitute Tools such as Stalking on Cue
- Playing Predation Substitute Games such as the Stalking Game

Functional reinforcers for dogs that like to chase:

- Playing Predation Substitute Games such as Backtracking
- Playing The Chase Game with a treat, toy or prey dummy

Functional reinforcers for dogs that like to grab-bite:

- Playing Predation Substitute Games such as Backtracking
- Playing The Chase Game with a treat, toy or prey dummy
- Playing Tug or Fetching a Treat tossed into the air

Functional reinforcers for dogs that like to possess:

- Playing Predation Substitute Games such as Backtracking
- Playing The Chase Game with a treat, toy or prey dummy

Functional reinforcers for dogs that like to dissect:

- Playing Predation Substitute Games such as Killing the Paper Bag
- Stuffing Carton Boxes, paper bags, wrapping paper or toilet rolls with treats and letting the dog rip them apart

- Engaging them in Problem-Solving Toys, such as stuffed Kongs, lickimats, food puzzles etc

Functional reinforcers for dogs that like to consume:

- Playing Predation Substitute Games, such as Backtracking and Free Search with a prey dummy, allowing them to eat treats out of the dummy
- Playing The Chase Game, the Sausage Tree Game or Killing the Paper Bag
- Scattering Treats in the grass or in fallen leaves.

Part 4: Interrupting Unwanted Predatory Behaviour

At some point, you will certainly have an unexpected encounter with wildlife when you're out and about. In case your dog goes over threshold, you have to interrupt your dog from performing parts of the predatory sequence that are either dangerous for them or another animal. This is why you need an emergency cue.

Your emergency cue should be used for encounters with other animals that appear very suddenly, or, they are very close to you. Examples could include; a cat running out from under a car as you walk past, a rabbit suddenly appearing from long grass in the field you are in, a deer quickly running across the woodland path you are on, etc. In situations like this, it's vital you interrupt your dog's predatory behaviour to prevent harm to them or the other animal. A reaction like this is very impulsive for your dog, so to expect them to not behave this way and simply ignore the animal is impossible, no matter how much time and effort you have put into their training. However, this is why you have worked on your emergency cues, exactly for instances like this one, to get you out of a tricky situation.

In another of my books, 'Rocket Recall' we look in depth at how to teach your dog a super strong recall which is used in situations where your dog is off leash, a fair distance away from you and they begin to chase an animal that has suddenly appeared. This special type of recall is designed to get your dog to abort their chasing mission and return back to you. Teaching your dog this can be complex, hence why there is a separate book dedicated to it. So, I will not go into great detail about this here, but you can take a sneak peek into Rocket Recall at the end of this book .

However, an emergency cue we will discuss here is the 'emergency exit' which is designed to work when your dog is close to you, on leash or off leash but close by, and an animal appears suddenly. It's essentially a U-turn to get you out of the situation.

We will also look at teaching your dog a 'hand touch' which can help you determine if your dog is still in a thinking state while you are working together.

As we discussed at the beginning of this book, predation is very hard to interrupt: we're not only fighting against genetics, but we're also dealing with a primal brain that handles instinctive dog behaviour and basic emotions.

The only way to get a foot in the door is to push into the same part of the primal brain, and this is where classical conditioning comes into play. By classically conditioning a cue, we anchor this cue directly in the part of the dog's brain where emotions happen. Once it is well-established and reinforced through repetition, the dog will follow this cue in a whiplash–like reaction, without even thinking about it first.

Note: When To Use Each Emergency Cue

If your dog is far away from you, notices wildlife, and starts to chase it, you will need to use your 'Rocket Recall' cue.

If your dog is close to you, either on or off leash, and notices wildlife, you will need to use your 'Emergency Exit' cue.

If you need to check if your dog is in a thinking state, while you are working through your PST exercises, you will need to use your 'hand touch' cue.

The Emergency Exit

The Emergency Exit is a positive interrupter that works through classical conditioning.

A positive interrupter is any behaviour that is incompatible with the unwanted behaviour and has been conditioned by positive reinforcement.

In the Emergency Exit, the dog learns to turn away from a trigger in a U-turn and to increase the distance between themself and the trigger. In order to ensure success even in the face of a full chase, you'll need an instantaneous reaction from your dog, and that means a lot of practice using high-value, versatile, and functional rewards.

Think about what your dog wants when they are chasing prey, and how you can functionally reward your dog for calling off a chase. Using these reinforcements to reward your Emergency Exit means that performing the Emergency Exit gets the same function for your dog as the chase itself: you are effectively "rewiring" that motivation in their brain from something you can't control (their natural instinct towards predation) to something you can control (their reactions to your proactive stimuli and cues).

Functional rewards for breaking off a chase could be:

- Throwing a toy or a ball
- Playing the Chase Game
- Sending your dog to Backtrack
- Throwing a paper bag stuffed with treats
- Playing tug-of-war with a rope or toy

Whenever you use the Emergency Exit to end the fun and to interrupt your dog's predation in a real-life situation, make sure you follow through afterwards. After using it, you'll need to practice at least ten times to "recharge" your dog's high expectations and the positive feelings that are linked to the Emergency Exit by practising and heavily rewarding the Emergency Exit in a non-distractive environment.

The Emergency Exit: The Protocol

The Emergency Exit: Step 1

Start with your dog walking beside you on leash. Give the verbal cue "This way." Wait a moment for your dog to process, then lure your dog into a 180° U-turn around you with a super yummy treat or an exciting toy in your hand. As soon as the 180° U-turn is complete, toss the treat or the toy into the direction that you are now heading in. Praise your dog enthusiastically, and repeat the process several times.

The Emergency Exit: Step 2

Start with your dog walking beside you on leash. Give the verbal cue "This way." Wait a moment for your dog to process, then lure your dog into a 180° U-turn with an EMPTY hand. As soon as the U-turn is complete, reach into your bag and toss a super yummy treat or toy into the direction that you are now heading in. Praise your dog enthusiastically.

The Emergency Exit: Step 3

Start with your dog walking beside you on a long line or off leash. Give the verbal cue "This way." As the dog turns around 180°, turn around as well and throw a super yummy treat or exciting toy into the direction that you are now both heading in. Praise your dog enthusiastically.

Special Tip:

Generalise the behaviour in various locations, gradually increasing the off-leash distance between you and your dog before giving the verbal cue. Carefully add distractions and only increase one area of distraction at a time. Your aim is a whiplash-like reaction from your dog, and that will need to be built up with patience on your part.

STEP 3

STEP 4

The Hand Touch

The hand touch is a "positive interrupter" like the Emergency Exit, but it works differently. The hand touch is a learned, or "operant" behaviour. Instead of classical conditioning that wires directly into your dog's emotions, the hand touch instead involves areas of the brain that are responsible for cognitive reasoning.

You can use the hand touch in any situation in which your dog needs to go from an emotional state back into a thinking state. With a hand touch, you can interrupt the predatory sequence and increase the distance to the trigger before allowing your dog to resume progression. Although you can use it to completely interrupt the predatory sequence, it is more skillfully employed as a tool for gentle readjustment away from the giving-chase threshold. The Hand Touch can be very useful when training Predation Substitute Tools, such as Stalking on cue. You can use it to bring some distance between your dog and the trigger without interrupting their hunting mode altogether.

Hand Touch: The Protocol

Hand Touch: Step 1

Put a treat between your ring finger and middle finger, or between your middle finger and index finger, and stretch out your hand. Present your hand in a way that allows your dog to touch your palm with their nose, reaching the treat that is stuck between your fingers. As soon as you feel your dog's nose on your palm, mark and release the treat. Repeat several times.

Hand Touch: Step 2

Stretch out your hand, this time without a treat between your fingers. As your dog will assume that there is a treat stuck between your fingers, they will still touch your palm with their nose. As soon as you feel your dog's nose on your palm, mark and get a treat out of your treat pouch. Feed them this treat from the same hand their nose just touched. Repeat several times until your dog reliably performs the hand touch.

Hand Touch Step 3

Stretch out your hand. As soon as your dog's nose touches your palm, say the verbal cue "Touch," get out a treat, and feed it to them from the same hand. Repeat several times.

Hand Touch Step 4

Say the verbal cue "Touch", wait a moment, then stretch out your palm. As the dog's nose touches your palm, mark and feed them a treat from the same hand.

Special Tips:

Generalise the behaviour in various locations, gradually increasing the off-leash distance between you and your dog before giving the verbal cue. Carefully add distractions and only increase one area of distraction at a time. Your aim is a whiplash-like reaction from your dog, and that will need to be built up with patience on your part.

The End Of The Book – The Beginning Of Your Predation Substitute Training Journey

Electric shock collars were banned in Germany in 2006. Once the "quick and easy fix" had been banned in a country famous for Europe's highest wildlife density, dog trainers and behaviourists had to get creative. They needed to collectively come up with more ideas to stop dogs from hunting. In response to this need, the Predation Substitute Training protocol started the first steps of its development.

While it is by no means a magic wand that compels your dog to abandon their predatory instincts, it goes beyond force, aversives, and quick fixes for lasting results. When dealing with predation, genetically-anchored patterns will always be at work, so it's just as important to acknowledge them as it is to try course-correcting them. This is precisely why management will always play a big part in predation protocol.

It is my hope that this training manual has given you all the tools that you will need to successfully harness your dog's predatory instincts without using intimidation, pain, or fear:

HUNTING TOGETHER

- You now understand what predation is and why your dog loves hunting so much.
- You have Predation Substitute Tools at hand, which means you can functionally reinforce your dog to stop and control themselves by letting them stalk or scan.
- You are now equipped with several need-oriented Predation Substitute Games to create a safe outlet for your dog's predatory energy, such as the Free Search, Backtracking, The Chase Game, the Stalking Game, the Sausage Tree and Killing the Paper Bag.
- You know how to put in place a safety net to immediately interrupt predatory chasing with the "Emergency Exit" and Hand Touch cues.

By hunting together instead of playing the role of interrupter and fun-spoiler, your relationship with your dog will improve, your connection will deepen, and the time you spend together will ultimately be even more rewarding.

Whether you train your dog in a purely positive way or follow a balanced approach to dog training and want to reduce punishment, I encourage you to give Predation Substitute Training a try. You will be amazed at how far motivation-based and need-oriented training will bring your canine companion.

I wish you and your dog happy training!

132

Malinka and Nanook

Acknowledgements

This book would not have been possible without my amazing trainer colleagues:

- Claire Staines from Lothlorien Dog Services in Scotland, my dear friend and mentor from whom I was allowed to learn, and through whom I still keep on learning. Claire, you are an inspiration!
- Lhanna Dickson for putting time and thoughts into this protocol, both by editing it and developing it into a new, exciting direction that will give us even more food for thought!
- A big shout out to the whole Lothlorien Team for your ongoing support and for making me feel close to you, even though I'm actually quite far away.

Special Thank Yous Go Out To:

- Sonja Rupp, for the lovely photos of my dogs performing PST.
- Charlotte Garner, Canine Author for the help with the second edition. (Visit Charlotte's website: https://charlotte-garner.com)
- Delany Martinez, WordChick for giving the first edition of my text a good polish.

- Päivi Kokko for the wonderful sketches (https://fitnsniff.fi/sketchnotes/)
- Beautiful Ori and her guardian for the amazing cover photo that was taken by Ann-Christin Mundsahl from https://ann-christin-mundsahl-fotografie.de/
- Fee Ketelsen for her sharp eye and helpful advice.

I want to mention at least some of the colleagues that paved the way for force-free, science-based predation protocols that I rely on in this training program:

- Dr. Ute Blaschke Berthold, a visionary trainer and behaviourist.
- Anja Fiedler, who recently merged and perfected several protocols in her comprehensive training program "Jagdverhalten – verstehen, kontrollieren, ausgleichen". If you read German, this is a must-read!
- Grisha Steward, whose book and training program BAT 2.0 heavily influenced the leash handling in this book. BAT 2.0 is the best resource out there if you're looking for a mindful way to handle your dog.

The biggest thank you is to my husband Kai for his ongoing support, his patience, and for always listening to me going on about dogs and training.

Last but not least, this book is dedicated to my dogs Malinka, Nanook, and Isla, my best teachers and closest companions.

About the Author

Simone Mueller, MA is a certified dog trainer and dog behavior consultant (ATN) from Germany.

She specializes in force-free anti-predation training and is the author of the Predation Substitute Training series: "Hunting Together", "Rocket Recall" and "Don't Eat That".

Simone is proud to be an Associate Trainer at the Scotland-based Lothlorien Dog Training Club (AT-LDTC) and a member of The Initiative of Force-Free Dog Training, the Pet Professional Guild (PPG) and the Pet Dog Trainers of Europe (PDTE).

Learn more at http://www.predation-substitute-training.com

Follow Simone's work on Facebook and Instagram:
facebook.com/predationsubstitutetraining
instagram.com/predation_substitute_training
#predationsubstitutetraining

Simone with Nanook and Isla

Courses

Would you like to delve deeper into the games and exercises of Predation Substitute Training and how you can help your to dog channel his predatory motivation in a healthy way?

On my website you can find a growing number of live and pre-recorded courses, including a comprehensive Predation Subsitute Training self-learning course.

Check out https://predation-substitute-training.com/courses

One Final Note

If, after reading and following this training program you feel like PST will never work for your dog, write me an email! Yes, I'm entirely serious - humans need to learn and adapt just as much as their canine companions and your take on the results will help me refine my approach(es) for the future.

If, on the other hand, you liked this training program and think that this is a game-changer in the relationship with your dog, please let the world know by leaving a rating and review on Amazon!

I ask this because reviews are the lifeblood of any independent book on Amazon. Without stars and reviews, there's a better-than-average chance you wouldn't have found this training program in the first place. Please take thirty seconds of your time (or potentially even less than that!) to support me as an independent author by leaving a rating.

If you would click five stars after the last page on your Kindle device or visit the link below and leave a positive review on Amazon, I would deeply appreciate it.

Click Account & Lists in the upper right corner -> Your Account -> Orders -> scroll down your orders and then click the Write a Product Review button on the right.

It's a bit hidden, but by doing this, your review will be a "Verified Purchase", and this carries far more weight.

After all, a quick rating or review helps me to provide my dogs with more toys and treats and honestly, which dog in the world doesn't deserve more toys and treats?

Thank you and happy training!
Simone

The Parts of the Predation Substitute Training Puzzle

ROCKET RECALL

FOR DOGS WHO
LOVE TO CHASE

FOR DOGS WHO
LOVE TO SCAVENGE

HUNTING TOGETHER

DON'T EAT THAT!

If your dog loves to chase wildlife, you have chosen a great place to start by reading Hunting Together! The information found here is one part of the holistic approach that forms Predation Substitute Training (PST). Understanding and implementing the entire Predation Substitute Training protocol will help you achieve better, longer-lasting results. The next part of the PST series is 'Rocket Recall.'

What is a "Rocket Recall?"

Imagine your dog is running at full speed towards a road, you need something that is guaranteed to get them to turn around and run towards you and away from danger instead.

All dogs need a reliable recall, it's an essential life skill and perhaps the most important thing you can teach your dog. Having a great recall helps to give your dog more freedom and keeps them safe in the process.

You will learn how to successfully navigate scenarios like these by teaching your dog their very own Rocket Recall. Just think how great it will feel when your dog runs happily back to you when you call them, instead of you chasing after them while they ignore you completely!

And, because I know how important it is that you know how to teach a fantastic recall to your dog, this is why I have dedicated a whole book solely to helping you achieve this with your dog.

'Rocket Recall' is part of my Predation Substitute Training series of books but also works independently for many other situations.

Would you like a reading sample?

Then turn the page and learn more about the how to teach your dog a Rocket Recall!

Rocket Recall

Why Do So Many Dog Owners Struggle With Their Dog's Recall?

A reliable recall is one of the greatest challenges for many dog owners. But why is that so?

First of all, we need to understand that a recall is something aversive - negative - that is happening to the dog. It's something that goes against what they actually want to do in the moment. When we use a recall, we're asking them to turn away and abandon something that they are interested in, or something they want to check out.

Turning away from that interesting smell, person, animal, or other distraction and having to come back to us is the first "disappointment" for the dog. We naturally try to "make up" for this disappointment by giving them a treat, but often, the treat is not really a reward for our dog. Why is this? It's because the treat doesn't fulfill a need that they feel at that moment. Giving a treat is not functional - it's not part of an understood system driven by their instincts - and it can become a second "disappointment" during the recall.

Let's look at it another way, for clarity. Think back and remember the way you felt as a child when a parent called you inside for dinner, but the other kids you were with kept on playing. While you likely enjoyed eating as a normal activity, in this situation, it wasn't what you actually wanted to do. You wanted to remain playing with your friends! You may have even perceived it as a kind of punishment, as you had to leave your friends behind. You felt disappointed, sad, maybe even angry that you had to abandon what you wanted to do, even though it was for something else that you typically enjoyed.

A dog that turns away from chasing a cat, or playing with another dog, might feel the same way, even if we offer them a treat. Even though your dog loves to eat at home and in a non-distracting environment, they might not perceive that same treat as a reward when outside the home. Believe it or not, this is one of the reasons why so many dogs are hesitant or even resistant to taking treats outside.

Exploring the idea of "disappointments" within a recall further, some dog owners struggle with their dog's recall because they consciously or unconsciously punish their dog for coming back. This may look like:

- A prior loss of temper and subsequent yelling at a "naughty" dog that slipped their lead or got out.
- A waver or hardness to your voice, born out of fear that they won't come back the last few steps or may dart into the road.
- Your body language and stance changing to a threatening one when you're preparing to chase your dog down as they turn away.

Even if you don't remember doing any of these things exactly, human nature dictates you're likely guilty of at least one at some point. It was when this happened that your dog may have started to associate your recall with something negative or punitive – the "disappointment." You recalled your dog from something interesting, put them on lead, or called them away from their friends and ended the fun. According to learning theory, this is punishment.

A final familiar reason why dogs struggle to come back is a lack of training. They may understand what a recall is functionally, in the moment, but not that recall means recall regardless of the situation. Their owners have trained their recall at home, or in a similar non-distracting environment, but neglected to instill proper generalisation of the cue. In order to generalise the cue properly, you'll need to repeat it hundreds, even thousands, of times in various situations and alongside different distractions.

In order to set our dogs up for success we need to carefully structure these situations and scaffold the distractions, allowing us to work through them in a kind of "bucket list" for our dogs. In this holistic training program, we will tackle all three of the common issues that cause dog owners to struggle with their dog's recall: the reluctance to abandon something interesting, a feeling of punishment, and a lack of training. We'll also learn how to make a reward functional, ensuring it has the intended effect on your dog and doesn't feel like a disappointment.

Throughout this training, you will play games with your dog that rewire their brain, ensuring that coming back to you is no longer a punishment. Once you've properly implemented these techniques, in fact, they'll actually feel the desire to come back to you. We'll also work together to create a well-structured and scaffolded bucket list of distractions, situations and reward options to work through. Let's get started!

Rocket Recall by Simone Mueller is available as e-book (ISBN 978-3-9821878-9-1), paperback (ISBN 978-3-9821878-8-4) and hardcover (ISBN 979-8393446840).

Do you have a "Hoover Dog"?

If you have a dog who loves to scavenge and you want to learn how to manage this successfully without using force or aversive methods. 'Don't Eat That!' is full of useful information about how to keep your dog safe by stopping them from scavenging and eating food they find on the ground. As you will discover, this is done by providing your dog with suitable scavenging outlets, instead of trying to eliminate this behaviour from their life entirely. This approach provides you with much more sustainable results than you would be able to achieve if you tried to stop your dog from showing this behaviour completely.

Are you curious why dogs love to scavenge?

Here's a reading sample!

Don't Eat That

Why Do Dogs Love To Scavenge?

The fact you are reading this book means there is a high chance that you already know that dogs love to scavenge! But you might be surprised to learn that there are several deep-rooted reasons for this; it's not as simple as them just feeling hungry or being greedy! Understanding why your dog loves scavenging so much can help you better work out how to manage this behavior successfully.

So, here are the reasons why your dog values scavenging so highly:

Scavenging Is A Basic Need For Your Dog

Something that every species of living beings rely upon is finding food. This is essential to their survival and is no different for our dogs. Although our domesticated pet dogs no longer rely on scavenging as their only way of finding food, it is often still something they naturally desire and feel the need to do.

Your Dog Is Simply Hungry

This is perhaps the most common reason which comes to mind when owners are faced with a scavenging dog! Many think their dog is doing it to be greedy, but in actual fact, they may be hungry. Some modern-day dog foods don't satisfy your dog's hunger for long, so when they come across something tasty on the ground, it can be tough for them to resist, even if it's something potentially harmful to them. Consider the type and amount of food your dog is getting, and how often they are fed over the day. Making changes to these things can be a good starting point for reducing your dog's scavenging, although it won't eliminate it completely! Even dogs who are fed high-quality foods can still find the temptation of some 'freebies' too difficult to ignore! Try feeding your dog a handful of food around 20 minutes before you go for a walk. Do this for a week and see if this can reduce their scavenging urges.

Dogs Find Scavenging Intrinsically Reinforcing

There are two things at play here that make scavenging intrinsically reinforcing for our dogs - their seeking and play systems. The seeking system is the most addictive of the two and can be likened to people who enjoy gambling. Although they don't win every time they take part, the thrill of the possibility of winning keeps them coming back for more again and again. They invest increasing amounts of time, energy, and concentration in anticipation of a win that might happen, in exactly the same way a human would when playing on slot machines or placing bets. When your dog wins by finding something to eat on the floor, the feeling of euphoria and excitement, along with the Dopamine that is released into their system, makes them want to scavenge again.

The play system means that scavenging feels good for your dog, they enjoy it, and it makes them happy! Your dog's enjoying the searching, finding, sniffing, chewing, licking, eating, and swallowing aspects of scavenging food. This releases feel-good endorphins into your dog's system, leaving them happy, satisfied, and relaxed. It's not hard to see why they would want to repeat this process as often as possible so that they can feel this way more often! This is similar to how humans feel when we have a lavish 3-course meal. We feel indulged and will look forward to the next opportunity we have to experience this.

Scavenging Is Genetically Anchored Into Your Dog

Wolves first started spending time closer to humans because they realized there was food near them that was easily accessible. Humans created waste and stored food, which was much easier for the wolves to scavenge from than trying to hunt and kill their own food. This relationship turned out to be mutually beneficial as the wolves deterred other animals and intruders from getting too close to the humans. This sparked the start of evolution from wolves to the dogs we know and love today.

Some wild dogs still live in a very similar way to their ancestors, living on the outskirts of villages and scavenging from what the villagers leave behind. Some breeds still retain these strong instincts to scavenge, even though they no longer depend on it for their survival.

Your Dog Is Used To Needing To Scavenge

The saying 'old habits die hard' is relevant to dogs who have been used to needing to scavenge to survive. Dogs that have lived on the streets, often for several months, need to scavenge food to eat. This could be hunting and killing animals, or the easier route for them is scavenging food that humans leave behind. In fact, their whole life will have been structured around finding food, and it will have taken up a large part of each day for them. They will have practised their scavenging skills to make them excellent at finding things to eat, so they are not wasting precious time and energy searching for food. So, it can be tough for them to stop suddenly, even if their new lifestyle no longer requires them to do it.

Boredom Can Make Your Dog Scavenge More

This is particularly common in breeds with high intelligence and energy levels. If they're not provided with enough mental and physical stimulation, your dog may start using scavenging to remedy their boredom. This gives them something fun and rewarding to do. So, it's important to ensure your dog's mental and physical needs are met, before you start this training protocol. Without this, the training won't be as effective.

Over-aroused Dogs Tend To Scavenge More

Dogs that are stressed, anxious, or over-aroused can use scavenging as a way to distract themselves and make themselves feel better. Dogs that are reactive towards other animals, people, and new scenarios can be more likely to resort to scavenging to try and help them feel more in control and calmer. If you think that your dog is scavenging because of underlying stress, or to try and distract themselves from stressful situations, it's best to contact a force-free trainer or behaviorist for advice prior to starting this training protocol.

Your Dog Is Searching For A Novel Taste

Humans tend to be creatures of habit, and we like to stick with what we know. So often, once we find a food that suits our dog, we stick with the same flavor, day after day, month after month. Although this might be the most convenient option for us, it is by far the most boring option for our dogs! Unless they suffer from allergies or intolerances, our dogs can benefit from having a wide selection of different flavors and protein sources in their diet. Whether they are raw fed, kibble fed, or you cook at home for them, so long as their diets are complete, nutritious, and tasty for them, that is the main thing! It will quickly become monotonous if dogs constantly eat the same food for extended periods. This can lead to them having a stronger urge to scavenge in a desperate bid to find something different and more exciting to eat!

Artificial Selection Can Increase Scavenging

The artificial selection of certain breeds can increase the likelihood and frequency of their scavenging behavior. This is regularly shown in members of the hound family, who are bred to live and work in large packs of other hounds. Many working hounds live in a large group and are fed together, meaning it's in their best interest to find, grab and eat the food as quickly as possible, to make sure they get a decent amount. Those that are not as fast, will get little to no food and will be hungry, so it's beneficial for them to refine their scavenging skills to become more successful at it.

Also, some gundog breeds like the Labrador, Flat Coated Retriever, and Golden Retriever have been found to be missing part of or all of the gene known as POMC. The Proopiomelanocortin gene (POMC) gene affects appetite, food motivation, fat storage, and, most importantly, satiety. Satiety signals when your dog is full; without this signal working correctly, which is the case with dogs with the faulty POMC gene, they won't know that they feel full. So, they will continue to eat more, even though they have had enough! This can understandably increase their scavenging, as they constantly feel hungry, even if they are well-fed and nourished.

Your Dog May Have A Medical Condition

If your dog is an excessive scavenger, or has recently started scavenging much more than usual, it is best to get them checked thoroughly by your vet to rule out any potential medical issues before you begin training. If your dog's scavenging is due to a medical condition, then this training protocol won't be successful until your dog has received the appropriate treatment to cure or manage their condition effectively. Conditions like gastroenteritis, gastritis, heartburn, indigestion, pancreatitis, acid reflux, IBD, and parasites can all increase scavenging because your dog is looking for something to make themselves feel more comfortable or to ease their symptoms.

Don't Eat That by Simone Mueller is available as e-book, paperback (ISBN 979-8359637954) and hardcover (979-8368381244)

Printed in Great Britain
by Amazon

44135715R00089